THE INQUIRING EYE
American Paintings

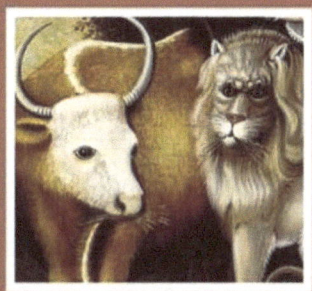

National Gallery of Art, Washington

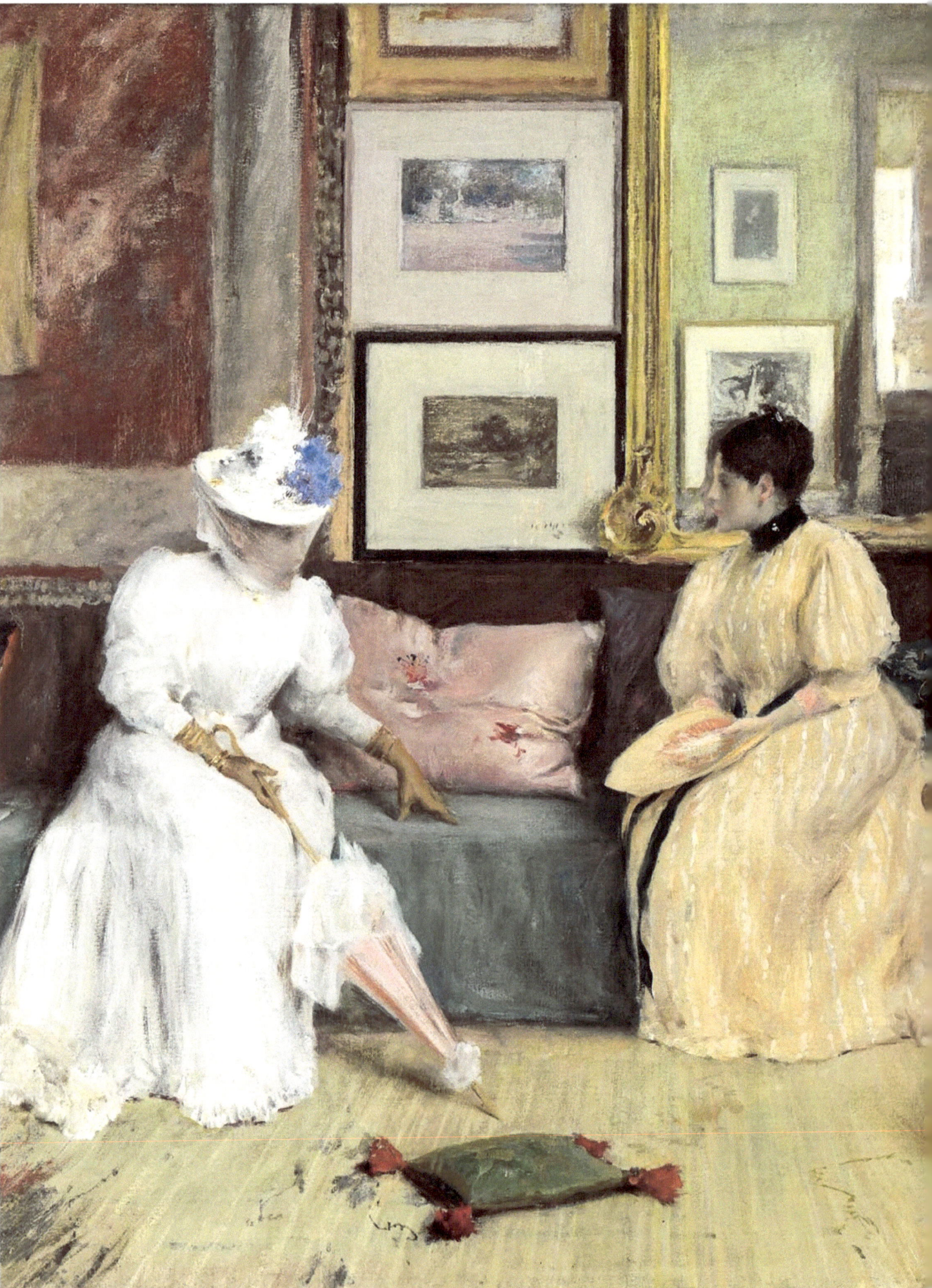

Goals	**Introduce the development of painting in America** from the mid-seventeenth to the early twentieth century
	Discuss the historical and cultural context within which this art was created
	Suggest discussion questions and activities that teachers can adapt to the needs and interests of their students

Components	**American Art at a Glance:** key ideas and issues summarized
	Historical Context: background and historical information on the development of American art
	Object Descriptions: specific information on the twenty American paintings from the National Gallery of Art reproduced in this packet
	Discussion Questions and Activities: teaching suggestions for classroom use
	Bibliography: annotated reading list for an expanded study of American art
	Timeline: covering the period spanned by the artists represented (c. 1760–c. 1914)
	Twenty Slides: the paintings discussed here from the National Gallery of Art collection
	Twelve Color Reproductions: selected from the twenty paintings

Acknowledgments   This text was prepared by William Kloss for the Department of Teacher
and School Programs, Education Division, and produced by the Editors Office.
© 1992 Board of Trustees, National Gallery of Art, Washington, D.C.

COVER: Edward Hicks, *Peaceable Kingdom*, c. 1834 (detail), National Gallery of Art,
Washington, Gift of Edgar William and Bernice Chrysler Garbisch
PAGE 2: William Merritt Chase, *A Friendly Call*, 1895 (detail), National Gallery of Art,
Washington, Chester Dale Collection
PAGE 6: George Inness, *The Lackawanna Valley*, 1855 (detail), National Gallery of Art,
Washington, Gift of Mrs. Huttleston Rogers
PAGE 38: Rembrandt Peale, *Rubens Peale with a Geranium*, 1801 (detail), National Gallery of
Art, Washington, Patrons' Permanent Fund

CONTENTS

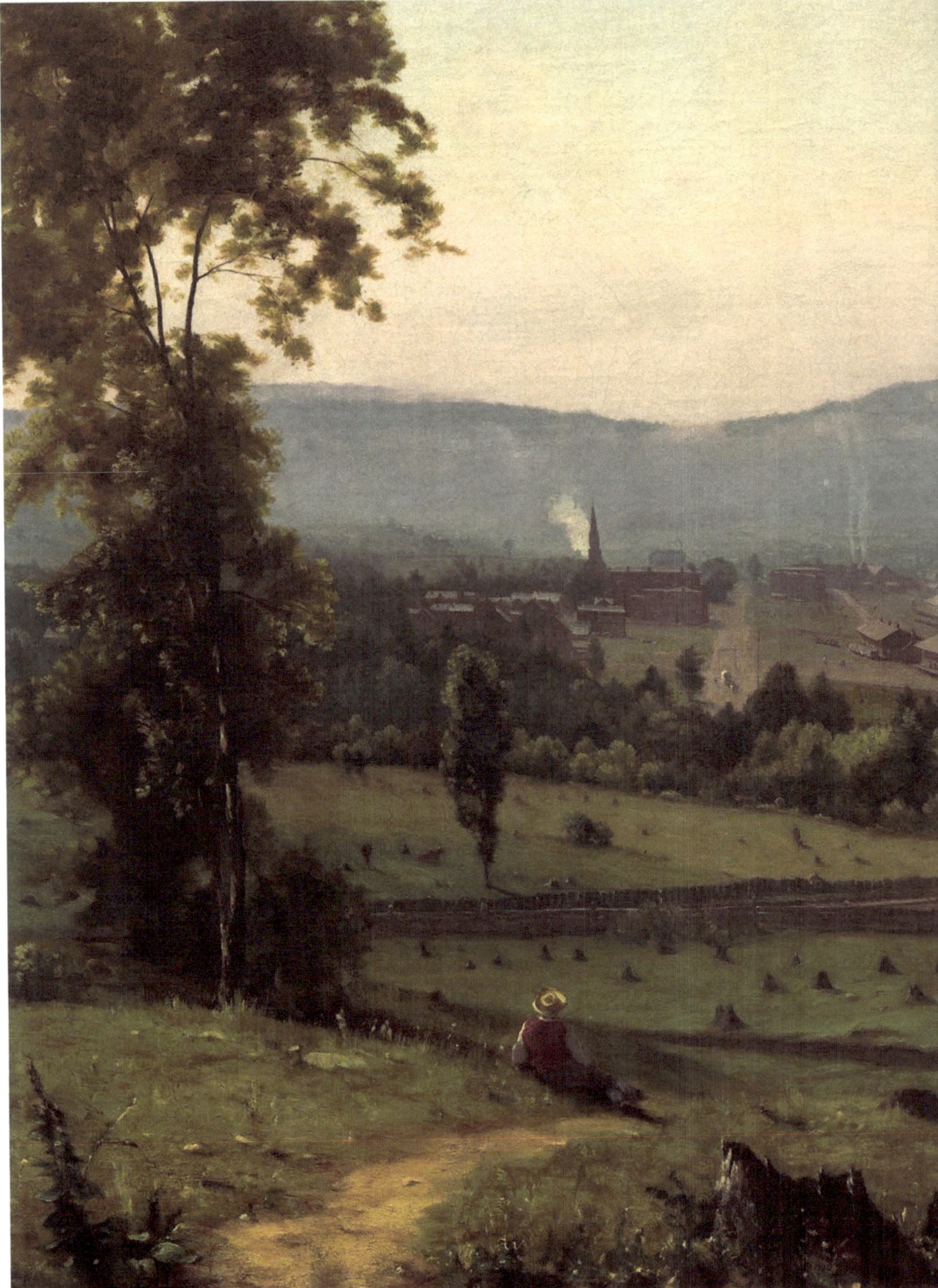

AMERICAN ART AT A GLANCE

The continent of North America was encountered by Europeans in a series of voyages over several centuries. These explorers returned with stories of a fabulous "New World," vast and rich in natural resources, which tempted other Europeans to establish settlements there in the 1600s. By the mid-1700s the colonies began to regard themselves as self-sufficient entities—the first step to independence and nationhood.

First Steps: Art in Colonial America

Artists who emigrated to the colonies worked in styles that reflected their native countries. These artists were rarely first-rate, and artists born in the colonies were often poorly trained. The English, who made up the majority of the colonists, preferred portraiture to other subjects, but colonial portraits became less aristocratic and more egalitarian in the harsher environment. Art was realistic and served a practical purpose. By the 1700s several renowned painters were active in the colonies, both immigrants and native-born. Still, it is estimated that only one in a hundred persons had his or her portrait painted in colonial America.

Finding Ourselves: Art in a New Nation

Portraiture remained the most popular subject in painting, especially to record the heroes of the American Revolution. The War of 1812 with Britain increased the pride and self-confidence of the new nation. Painters introduced new subjects to American art: historical pictures, landscape views, still lifes, stories from literature, and scenes from daily existence. More artists went to Europe to study great art of the past. Schools or academies of art and early museums were founded to provide technical training for artists and to increase public awareness and taste for the arts. But by the 1830s and 1840s civic and artistic optimism gave way to pessimism arising from the debate over slavery and the preservation of the Union.

American Landscape: Reality, Myth, and Symbol

Painters of the American landscape not only captured the appearance of the country but also expressed the significance it held for its citizens and commented on the progress of its society. They stressed the vast size of the continent, its special geographic features, and every characteristic that seemed to set it apart as specifically American. Paintings of the landscape addressed the confrontation between wilderness and civilization, between nature's pristine beauty and man's intervention. Landscape took the place of the mythologies of older countries and was personified and invested with moral significance. The imperialistic expansion to the Pacific by European settlers, regarded as "Manifest Destiny," or an inevitable course of events, was expressed in paintings of the awe-inspiring western landscape that made America seem a new paradise. The Civil War divided the land as it did the nation, and afterward artists painted the landscape with a profound stillness and with implicit references to biblical salvation and regeneration.

Ambition and Meditation: American Art Comes of Age

Prosperity and poverty contrasted sharply in the postwar era. Great fortunes and the celebrations of the nation's centennial in Philadelphia and the World's Columbian Exposition in Chicago gave rise to extravagant building projects. The center of political power shifted from the East to the Midwest and the West. Americans' desire for European culture resulted in the avid collecting of European art followed by a burst of museum-building in America. The latest stylistic innovations in art, such as the techniques of the French impressionists, were adopted by American painters. At the same time, social and political dissatisfaction darkened this "Gilded Age," and American art was often introspective. Disaffected artists escaped to exotic parts of the world. Art became less descriptive and more expressive of the artist's feelings. The century's end brought many doubts, as Americans faced the dark past of the Civil War and the unknowns of the modern world. Yet through these events America developed its own artistic tradition. The unique contributions of artists in the early twentieth century announced the growing maturity of American art.

HISTORICAL CONTEXT

American art developed simultaneously with the new society of the United States. Both were of European origin and introduced to the New World by European colonists. It is ironic that one studies "American" art as an offshoot of European art rather than of native American art. Primarily because the numerous American Indian tribes were not unified, they were unable to resist the advance of organized colonial forces throughout their lands, so America became Europeanized.

Although Europeans, notably the Norsemen, reached North America five hundred years before the voyages of Columbus, they established no permanent colonies and left few traces behind. During the Middle Ages and the Renaissance the desire for the spices and wealth of China, Japan, and India induced intrepid sailors, with the backing of their monarchs, to search for a direct route to the Orient across the ocean. Portuguese explorers of the fifteenth century greatly added to Europeans' knowledge of the world, but they never reached the mainland of North America. Neither did Columbus in his four voyages between 1492 and 1502, although his first brought him as close as the Bahamas and Cuba, which he thought was China! John Cabot, in the employ of the king of England, probably reached Newfoundland in 1497 and established the English claim to North America.

The sixteenth century brought colonization attempts by the Spanish, with the conquest of Mexico; by the French, with fur trading posts in what is now Canada; and by the English, in Virginia (1585). The Virginia colony disappeared (the "Lost Colony"), and only in 1607 was a new English colony established at Jamestown. It was followed by settlements at Plymouth (1620) and Massachusetts Bay (1628), and these became the first permanent English colonies of North America. The Dutch founded a colony with the purchase of Manhattan Island from Native Americans in 1626. It became New Amsterdam, the capital of the colony, until defeat by the English in 1664, when it became New York. In 1682 England granted the Quaker William Penn a large territory later called Pennsylvania.

The English colonists were thriving in what would become New England, the Middle Atlantic states, and the Carolinas. But the French colonists, with the help of Indian allies, fought for control of Canada and the Northeast. In addition to troops sent from England, the conflict involved the colonial residents as military participants. The culmination of the British-French struggle for supremacy in the Northeast and Canada was the series of battles known in Europe as the Seven Years' War (1756–1763) and known in the British colonies as the French and Indian Wars. The French frequently had the upper hand in these conflicts until the decisive and famous Battle of Quebec (1759), when the French were routed by the British forces.

During the colonial period relations between Great Britain and its colonies were not always smooth. The Massachusetts Bay Colony claimed the status of an independent commonwealth in 1652, and in Virginia settlers rebelled against the colonial governor (Bacon's Rebellion) in 1676. American exports were a sizeable part of Great Britain's trade, but the colonists received little of the profit. Then in the 1760s the British Parliament decided to impose import taxes on the American colonies: the Sugar Act, the Stamp Act, and taxes on tea, glass, and paper. The citizens responded with boycotts on the taxed items, and radicals responded with sabotage—the famous Boston Tea Party.

When the British Parliament passed the Coercive Acts in 1774, closing the port of Boston and revoking most of the chartered rights of Massachusetts, the colonies' First Continental Congress was convened in Philadelphia to demand that Britain repeal its taxes and return political autonomy to the colonies. When Parliament failed to satisfy American demands, the large British military force still maintained in America was inevitably drawn into local conflicts. At Concord "the shot heard round the world" (Ralph Waldo Emerson) was fired, and within a month the British fort at Ticonderoga had been captured by Ethan

Allen's "Green Mountain Boys." The Second Continental Congress assembled in May 1775, and the Continental army was hastily formed under the command of George Washington. His siege of Boston ended with the American occupation of Dorchester Heights, the first significant colonial victory. Four months later the Declaration of Independence was adopted, and though the revolutionary war would last seven years, the United States of America was born.

First Steps: Art in Colonial America

American art is older than the nation. The European colonists—settlers from Holland, Scandinavia, the Germanic lands, Spain, France, and England—left artistic legacies in different geographical areas of North America. Painters who emigrated to America brought their native styles with them. Those who were born here also emulated the European forms, though they had little knowledge of the established techniques taught in art schools abroad. But the prevalence of the English by the mid-eighteenth century guaranteed the adoption of its artistic tradition. It was a tradition less rich and varied than that of many other European nations. Dominated by aristocratic portraiture, British art had a secondary interest in landscape painting and scenes of daily life.

Portrait painting fit the needs and desires of the colonists, who were removed from the cosmopolitan life and the artistic tastes of the leisure class of London or other European cities. Engaged in the difficult task of making a living through trade or agriculture while building homes and communities, the North American settlers were willing to pay artists to record the likenesses of their families—"ourselves and our posterity," as it was afterward expressed in the Preamble to our Constitution. Therefore, the overwhelming number of paintings in America through the colonial period and beyond are portraits.

A portrait was often painted as a "remembrancer" of a seldom-seen relative or a deceased family member. In 1770 John Greenwood in London wrote to John Singleton Copley in Boston, asking him to paint a portrait of his mother, whom he had not seen in seventeen years, "as she now appears, with old age creeping upon her." This preference for realism in portraits, springing from the natural wish to know how one's parent or child actually looked (there was a high infant mortality rate) became the favored approach in American portraiture, in contrast to the idealized or "improved" portraits favored in England.

Most of the painters who chose to resettle in colonial America were not artists of the first rank. Otherwise, they would not have relinquished the more financially secure European support of the arts—except in cases where they were seeking political or religious freedom. But a second-rate immigrant artist still had the benefit of formal training in the techniques of painting, something that artists born in the colonies lacked unless they traveled abroad to acquire it. Despite this disadvantage, by the middle of the eighteenth century native-born painters of genius began to emerge. The finest were Robert Feke (c. 1707–1752), John Singleton Copley (1738–1815), and Charles Willson Peale (1741–1827).

Robert Feke, the details of whose career are obscure, followed the tradition of the itinerant artist, who went from town to town and city to city looking for portrait commissions. His strongest portraits are usually of men, whom he treated as powerful structural masses: ramrod straight bodies (often three-quarter length), a hand often planted firmly on a tabletop like a column base, the broad curve of a coat front sweeping up to a dignified, impassive head (see fig. 1). Such monumental dignity was rare in colonial portraiture before Feke.

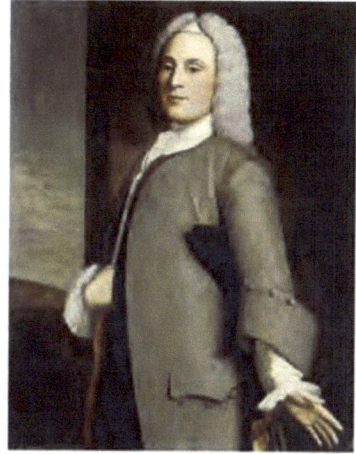

John Singleton Copley's colonial portraits display his remarkable concentration in studying and replicating the features of his sitters, yet his portraits also seem to reveal the sitter's inner character. No other artist so completely conveyed the resolute, thoughtful, self-reliant quality of the American colonists (see slide 1). Copley was torn between staying in Boston, where his reputation as the leading artist in New England brought him an excellent income, or going to Europe to improve his art by studying the great artists of the

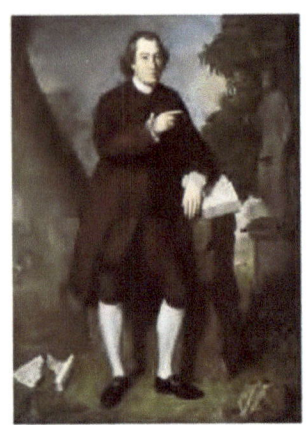

Fig. 2 Charles Willson Peale, *John Beale Bordley*, 1770, oil on canvas. National Gallery of Art, Washington, Gift of The Barra Foundation, Inc.

past and ancient Roman sculpture. "Were I sure of doing as well in Europe as here," he wrote, "I would not hesitate a moment in my choice, but I might in the experiment waste a thousand pounds and two years of my time, and have to return baffled to America" (see James Thomas Flexner, *The Double Adventure of John Singleton Copley* [Boston, 1969]). In 1774 Copley went to Europe, and when the Revolution made it impracticable to return, he settled in London for the rest of his life. There he acquired the thorough technical knowledge of painting that he could not receive in America and, though he was still capable of painting masterpieces, his style gradually became hard to distinguish from other talented European painters of the day.

Charles Willson Peale went to London from 1767 to 1769 to study with Benjamin West. West was from Pennsylvania but had long since settled in London. Although West became painter to the king and president of the Royal Academy, he retained a deep affection and sympathy for his birthplace, and for some forty years he welcomed and assisted American painters in London. After his course of study with West, Peale returned to the colonies. He was a man of enormous energies and enthusiasms—an inventor, a natural scientist, and the founder of a famous museum, the first systematic museum of natural history and art in America. A friend of George Washington, he became the first major painter of the leading citizens of the revolutionary and federal periods. Like Copley, Peale was aware that a thorough knowledge of classical sculpture was considered one "of the requisites of a good painter. These are more than I shall ever have time or opportunity to know, but as I have a variety of Characters to paint I must, as Rembrandt did, make these my antiques, and improve myself as well as I can while I am providing for my support" (see Lillian B. Miller, ed., *The Selected Papers of Charles Willson Peale* [New Haven, 1983]). In fact, he improved his art technically throughout his long career, while always retaining his most recognizable characteristic: an ability to paint his fellow citizens with expressions of frankness and affability (see fig. 2). To an unusual degree, viewers feel they know these people.

In their abilities and their attitudes toward art, Feke, Copley, and Peale are the most typical native-born artists of colonial America. They became technically skilled painters, and their work shows a deep understanding of human character. If their predecessors took the tentative first steps in American art, these three made great, confident strides and profoundly influenced succeeding generations.

Finding Ourselves: Art in a New Nation

Thomas Jefferson wrote in 1795: "We have chanced to live in an age which will probably be distinguished in history, for its experiments in government on a larger scale than has yet taken place. But we shall not live to see the result" (see Adrienne Koch and William Peden, eds., *The Life and Selected Writings of Thomas Jefferson* [New York, 1944]). Jefferson's keen awareness of the historical significance of the revolutions in America and France was shared by most Americans during the first generation under the new federal government.

The self-consciousness of this generation was also characteristic of the art and literature of the federal period (c. 1789–1829). American pride was reinforced by victory in the War

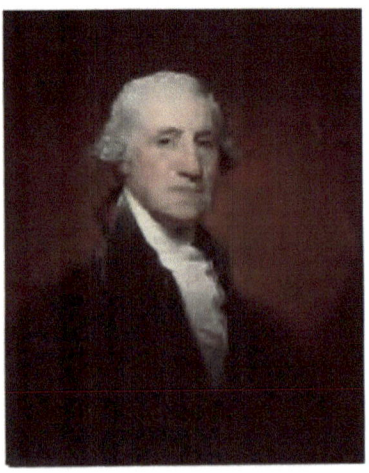

Fig. 3 Gilbert Stuart, *George Washington* [Vaughan-Sinclair portrait], 1795/1796, oil on canvas. National Gallery of Art, Washington, Andrew W. Mellon Collection

of 1812 (the "second war with Britain"), which culminated in the extraordinary triumph of General Andrew Jackson over the British forces at New Orleans. Portraiture was still the mainstay of American art, and artists such as Gilbert Stuart, John Trumbull, Thomas Sully, and Samuel F. B. Morse vied with the older Charles Willson Peale in painting the portraits of the heroes and statesmen of the nation. The public admiration of George Washington, in particular, was such that he was virtually deified by American artists. Stuart, for example, executed more than a hundred portraits of George Washington (see fig. 3).

Despite the instinctive realism of American portrait painters, there was now a tendency to idealize their subjects, attributable to the buoyant nationalism of this generation. While statesmen and leaders

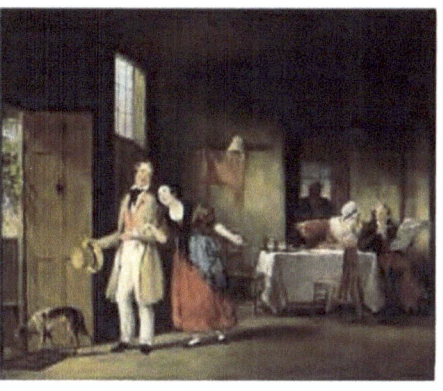

provided subjects for art, however, the federal government was unwilling to provide patronage for civic art. History painter John Trumbull produced a series of revolutionary war scenes, some of which were engraved for distribution to subscribers. All of the images were intended as models for larger paintings for which he sought commissions, especially from the federal government. But no official commission was forthcoming for more than three decades. In 1817 Congress at last asked Trumbull to produce four large paintings for the Capitol Rotunda. Other artists faced equal indifference in their attempts to create large-scale monuments to the Revolution or to democratic institutions, and this lack of support resulted in the failure of American history to become a popular subject in American art.

In the 1820s, however, a new subject did win widespread popularity, and many talented artists embraced it: landscape. The American landscape was a source of national pride and international wonder. A vast, unspoiled continent that stood in stark contrast to the overcrowded, "civilized" European landscape, it was likened to a "new Eden" offering a hope of moral regeneration.

Other subjects such as still-life painting also became increasingly popular. Although European still-life painting, especially in Holland, was influential in its emphasis on abundance, the roots of American still life may be found equally in decoration for furniture or wall paneling. Still life reflects an interest in one's home and possessions, and it tends to flourish in republican societies where the family holds an important position.

American literature—the vivid fiction of Washington Irving or the Leatherstocking novels of Fenimore Cooper, for instance—provided popular subjects for artists. When John Quidor painted *The Return of Rip Van Winkle* (see slide 9), he knew that his audience was familiar with the classic tale and would recognize the scene. During the 1830s and 1840s the number of paintings with literary references grew. The two arts matured together in America, with literature finding an admiring international audience long before painting.

Genre painting—scenes of daily life—emerged during the same decades, perhaps reflecting the frontier spirit of Jacksonian democracy. Genre subjects offered the artist opportunities to comment on social customs and foibles. The strong narrative strain in genre painting parallels that in popular literature. In fact, *The Bashful Cousin*, a genre painting by Francis William Edmonds, was probably inspired by a popular story of the day (see fig. 4).

Many artists at this time went abroad to travel and study in London and Paris or in Italy. One reason was to see the great monuments of Western art and to learn the techniques by which those masterpieces had been created. Another reason was to experience a culture where art was highly respected by an educated public who bought art and went to art exhibitions. The painter and inventor Samuel F. B. Morse wrote in a letter from London dated September 17, 1811, "in America [art] seemed to lie neglected, . . . but here it is the constant subject of conversation, and . . . no person is esteemed accomplished or well educated unless he possesses almost an enthusiastic love for paintings" (see William Kloss, *Samuel F. B. Morse* [New York, 1988]). Americans studying abroad during this period did not usually become expatriates but remained ardent patriots while soaking up the art they encountered everywhere in Europe. The cultural dialogue between America and Europe, which has persisted throughout this nation's history, was complicated by the apparent conflict between the American artists' democratic values and their desire for aristocratic patronage.

A growing support for the role of art in the new republic led to the founding of art academies, which provided for the instruction of artists, the exhibition of their work, and the refinement of public taste. The American Academy of the Fine Arts (long led by John Trumbull) was established in 1802; the Pennsylvania Academy of the Fine Arts opened in 1806; and the National Academy of Design (of which Samuel F. B. Morse was a founder and president) began in 1826. These academies reflected the increased confidence of American artists and a concerted effort to expand the patronage for their work. The euphoria and prosperity following the War of 1812 (called the Era of Good Feelings) seemed likely to improve the artistic climate. But economic reversals such as the financial panic of 1837 and, above all, the increasing regional tensions arising from slavery and economic disparities had an adverse effect. Artistic activity continued, but public and private patronage did not expand as hoped. The imminent storm of civil conflict and national disunion, greatly feared even by those who thought it inevitable, was seldom out of the national consciousness. Pessimism was widespread and was echoed by painters such as Thomas Cole and by writers such as Henry Wadsworth Longfellow: "Darker and darker / The black shadows fall; / Sleep and oblivion / Reign over all" (*Curfew*, 1846).

American Landscape: Reality, Myth, and Symbol

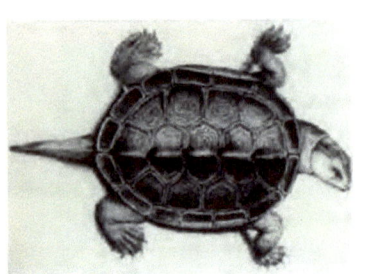

From the beginning of exploration and colonization the New World astonished the Europeans. New World phenomena were recorded in words and pictures, such as John White's memorable watercolors of plants, animals, and native inhabitants painted in 1585–1586 in the Roanoke colony of Virginia (see fig. 5). These were pictorial essays in natural history and anthropology, but they were also imbued with a sense of wonderment, as though the artist had found himself in the Garden of Eden.

By the time the United States came into being, Americans and Europeans alike had long been aware of the incredible vastness of the North American continent and its flanking oceans. As the new nation moved to incorporate the continent's entire breadth "from sea to shining sea," artists, writers, and natural scientists enthusiastically recorded the landscape and their response to it. Thomas Jefferson was among the first to describe at length some of the country's physical features in his *Notes On Virginia* (1784). Jefferson was a paragon of the Age of Reason, so it is fascinating to see how he interlaced facts with his psychological response to the Natural Bridge, a famous geological formation in Virginia:

The fissure, just at the bridge, is, by some admeasurements, two hundred and seventy feet deep, by others only two hundred and five. . . . Its breadth in the middle is about sixty feet . . . and the thickness of the mass, at the summit of the arch, about forty feet. . . . Though the sides of this bridge are provided in some parts with a parapet of fixed rocks, yet few men have resolution to walk to them, and look over into the abyss. You involuntarily fall on your hands and feet, creep to the parapet, and peep over it. Looking down from this height about a minute, gave me a violent headache.

As with portraiture, realism was the standard approach to depicting the land. Therefore, topographic landscapes, which describe surface details and appearance, were typical of the earliest landscape paintings. But as landscape became an important artistic subject by the 1820s, realism was often combined with artistic imagination and invention.

In a letter of 1826 to the great landscape painter Thomas Cole, his patron, Robert Gilmor of Baltimore, argued that as long as an artist "studied and painted from Nature . . . his pictures were pleasing, because the scene was real," and added, "I prefer real American scenes to compositions." Cole tactfully replied that "compositions are [not] so liable to be failures as you suppose. . . . If the Imagination is shackled, and nothing is described but what we see, seldom will anything truly great be produced, either in Painting or Poetry" (see Barbara Novak, *American Painting of the Nineteenth Century* [New York, 1969]).

Because the Appalachian mountain chain was a formidable barrier to westward expansion, it was the frontier for a long time. Thus Thomas Cole and his contemporaries painted primarily in the northeastern United States, along the Hudson River, or in the White Mountains, the Catskills, or the Adirondacks. This group of artists is called the Hudson River School. It was wilderness, but wilderness on the doorstep, and from his sketching trips Cole returned to his studio to paint his "compositions" of the American landscape. Although his paintings were often of specific, well-known sites, Cole and his colleagues sometimes chose to emphasize the American character of a scene with titles such as *American Lake Scene* (Cole) or *American Wilderness* (Asher B. Durand).

One of the most suggestive landscape themes, probably introduced by Cole, was the home in the wilderness. Paintings of this theme typically show a solitary log cabin in a clearing, close to a lake or river. The father of the pioneer family who lives here is often seen returning home, carrying fish or game. He is welcomed by his wife and children, smoke rises from the chimney, the wash is hanging out to dry. It is a peaceful scene, but the stumps

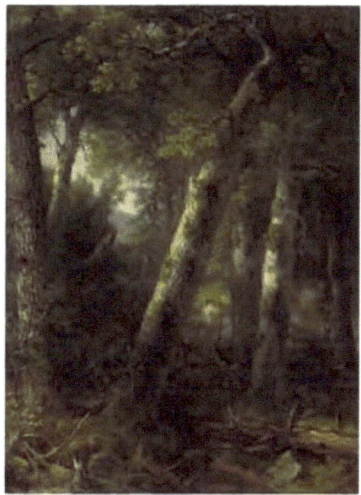

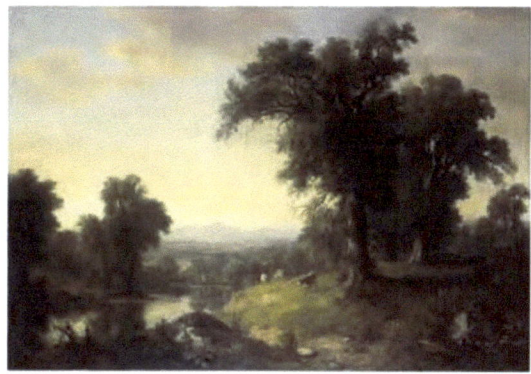

LEFT: Fig. 6. Asher B. Durand, *Forest in the Morning Light*, c. 1855, oil on canvas, National Gallery of Art, Washington, Gift of Frederick Sturges, Jr

ABOVE: Fig. 7. Asher B. Durand, *A Pastoral Scene*, 1858, oil on canvas, National Gallery of Art, Washington, Gift of Frederick Sturges, Jr

of the trees that were felled to build the home dot the foreground in sharp contrast to the seemingly endless wilderness immediately behind the dwelling (see slide 8). This is the confrontation of rudimentary civilization and the untamed wilderness, and it was a theme of such meaning to Americans in a still-uncharted continent that it continued to inspire artists for several generations.

Similarly, artists alternately painted scenes of cultivated pastures and valleys or forest interiors dense with rocks and trees and animated by streams and waterfalls (see figs. 6 and 7). The former, though showing signs of humanity's civilizing intervention, diminished the actual presence of people and often banished more disruptive signs of "progress" such as the railroad altogether. The latter not only were picturesque explorations of rugged forest landscape but sometimes—perhaps usually—carried implicit philosophical or moral meanings. In a famous essay on *Nature* (1836) Ralph Waldo Emerson wrote: "In the woods, we return to reason and faith. There I feel that nothing can befall me in life—no disgrace, no calamity (leaving me my eyes), which nature cannot repair."

It is difficult today to fully appreciate the deep emotional response to the northeastern American landscape expressed by painters, writers, and others. The English actress Fanny Kemble, who settled in America, visited the Hudson Highlands in 1832 and exclaimed: "I was filled with awe. The beauty and wild sublimity of what I beheld almost seemed to crush my facilities. . . . I felt as though I had been carried into the immediate presence of God" (see Raymond J. O'Brien, *American Sublime* [New York, 1981]). Inherent in such a rapturous response was the mystical notion of the ancientness of the landscape, especially its forests. Instead of the ancient gods of the Greeks or the Celts, America had its landscape, which could be personified as its own mythological deity. Thus Longfellow could write of "the forest primeval," where the "murmuring pines and the hemlocks . . . Stand like Druids of eld, with voices sad and prophetic," and of "the deep-voiced neighboring ocean," which "in accents disconsolate answers the wail of the forest" (*Evangeline*, 1847).

The ocean occupies a special place in America's "mythology." The early colonists were less likely to regard the Atlantic Ocean as a prospective avenue of international commerce than as a providential barrier between Europe (the old political and moral order) and America (the new order). The French visitor Alexis de Tocqueville wrote in 1835 that the protection of the ocean "would facilitate the maintenance of a democratic republic in the United States" (*Democracy in America* [London, 1835–1840]). The American poet James Russell Lowell memorably summed up this sentiment in 1848: "O my friends, thank your god, if you have one, that he / 'Twixt the Old World and you set the gulf of a sea" ("Cooper," in *A Fable for Critics*).

The fact that the country was so protected on both sides meant that for many Americans the two oceans became symbols of a special historical destiny, and thus the American landscape as a whole began to assume a more specifically nationalistic significance. Many paintings show American harbors bustling with vessels of commerce, but there are many

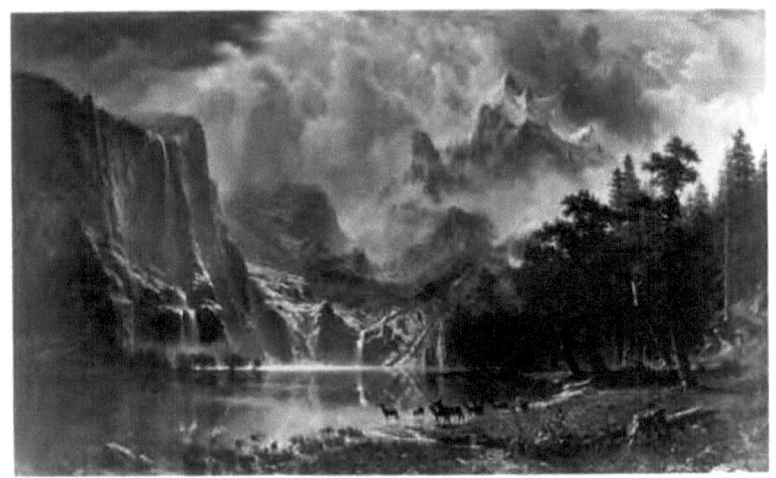

others in which the coast is largely uninhabited and the expanse of ocean outweighs any boats that may appear (see slide 11). They were painted for their own sake and also as reminders of their national significance. The country's great lakes and rivers were also interpreted—implicitly or explicitly—as symbols of regeneration and purification.

Myths and mysteries sprang from both forest and ocean, in the form of frontier legends, native American lore, tall tales, and works of literature. In addition to Irving's legends and Cooper's novels, other major American writings inspired by the forests and oceans (and lakes and rivers) include Longfellow's *The Song of Hiawatha*, Herman Melville's *Moby Dick*, Henry David Thoreau's *Walden*, and Mark Twain's *Huckleberry Finn*.

The approach of mid-century was accompanied by fears that the federal Union would dissolve. The decisive military victory in the Mexican War of 1846–1848 brought with it a temporary upswing in the national mood and an outpouring of paintings about the revolutionary period. The war was immediately followed by the California gold rush, an event of greater significance for the nation than simply that some individuals struck it rich. It created a considerable shift of the population westward, making it a land rush as much as a gold rush, and it renewed the appreciation of the abundance of America. With the Compromise of 1850, the United States Senate made one last effort to resolve the discord over slavery and economic disparity, but this only succeeded in delaying the schism.

The Civil War divided the nation for four horrible years, decimating its population of young men and passing on a legacy of bitterness that would persist for generations. Many Americans who moved West were motivated by an urgent need for healing and renewal. This revived the old dream of a new Eden, now on the other side of the continent. References to Eden, the promised land of the Old Testament (Exodus), or to the renewal of God's covenant with man after the biblical flood (Genesis) were common in paintings of the postwar period and attest to the need for healing.

The paintings of the western landscape that now appeared were inspired by such feelings and were in turn inspirational to those who had never seen the majestic, awesome prairies and canyons of the West, uniquely American wonders (see fig. 8). Already in 1834 William Cullen Bryant had written: "These are the gardens of the Desert, these / The Unshorn fields, boundless and beautiful, / For which the speech of England has no name— / The Prairies" ("The Prairies"). The concept of Manifest Destiny, that it was inevitable and right that the descendants of white European colonists should inhabit and govern the whole continent, grew during and after the war and gave added significance to paintings of the West.

Landscape painters throughout the country seemed compelled by the trauma of the war to seek a new landscape vision, a way of expressing the radically changed national consciousness. In painting after painting, a profound stillness is communicated. In others, blazing sunsets at once apocalyptic and benedictory stun the viewer (see slide 12). Symbolic images proliferate in postwar painting, such as the recurring "ship of state," which sometimes appears as a stranded or wrecked boat lying useless on the shore and at other times as a solitary ship sailing on expansive waters.

Fig. 8. Albert Bierstadt. *Among the Sierra Nevada Mountains, California*, 1868, oil on canvas. National Museum of American Art, Smithsonian Institution. Bequest of Helen Huntington Hull, granddaughter of William Brown Dinsmore, who acquired the painting in 1873 for "The Locusts," the family estate in Dutchess County, N.Y.

About 1880 landscape painting underwent a further development. A more personal, often highly subjective interpretation of landscape is apparent in paintings by Albert Pinkham Ryder, George Inness, and Winslow Homer. These works will be discussed in the next section, devoted to the last decades of the century and a profoundly changed America.

Ambition and Meditation: American Art Comes of Age

As America recovered from the trauma of the Civil War, the country was characterized by contrasting conditions and attitudes. The industrial strength of the northern states brought unparalleled prosperity, while the economic chaos of reconstruction in the southern states (1865–1877) left a legacy of poverty and distrust. The continent was rapidly opening up, and the completion of the first transcontinental railroad in 1869 marked the real integration of the western states and territories into the nation.

Great fortunes were made and spent in the ambitious postwar era, the so-called Gilded Age. The building of the Brooklyn Bridge (1869–1883), then the longest suspension bridge in America, captured the public imagination permanently as a strong yet graceful symbol of the new American city and its spirit of enterprise. The construction and decoration of the Library of Congress (1886–1897) during a period widely referred to as the American renaissance represented commitment to enlightenment in a democratic society. There were two great national celebrations—the centennial events in Philadelphia and the World's Columbian Exposition in Chicago (1893)—which were conceived both as reminders of America's happy beginnings and optimistic harbingers of a radiant future. One patriotic innovation was the pledge of allegiance, written in 1892, the quadricentennial year of Columbus' voyage of discovery, and presented to the public at the Columbian Exposition.

The Columbian Exposition itself was staged amid a vast array of neo-Roman architecture, a revival in a way of the classical Roman forms adopted for the United States Capitol and other public buildings a century earlier (see fig. 9). The Roman style had once and could still symbolize the Roman republic and Roman law, the models for American government. The architect Louis Sullivan, who disapproved of this style, nonetheless remembered that the "crowds [at the exposition] were astonished. . . . To them it was a veritable Apocalypse, a message inspired from on high" (see Hugh Morrison, *Louis Sullivan: Prophet of Modern Architecture* [New York, 1935]).

There was another sort of significance to the Columbian Exposition: its location. Chicago was now the great transportation hub of the continent. The Erie Canal was succeeded by the railroads, and for decades Chicago was almost the principal distribution point from which the abundant agricultural produce of the northern Mississippi Valley or meat from western cattle and Iowa hogs reached the East. This "City of the Big Shoulders" (1916), as Chicago's own Carl Sandburg later called it, had achieved a cultural vitality to match its commercial muscle, and it embodied the spirit of national renewal.

The great buildings of this American renaissance, both public and private, required decoration, and many painters and sculptors worked on the adornment of churches, courthouses, mansions, libraries, and museums. The art of stained glass was revived by Louis Comfort Tiffany and others for the production of quantities of windows and lamps. Mural paintings were much in demand.

The attraction of Europe grew strong once again, for newly wealthy American tourists and for ambitious artists. Many of the former brought paintings, sculpture, and objets d'art home from their travels, works that greatly influenced other collectors and the public generally. Many of these works of art eventually found their way into American museums, which had multiplied in the last third of the century. Artists who traveled abroad continued to study the great collections of old master paintings. After 1880, however, they also found themselves

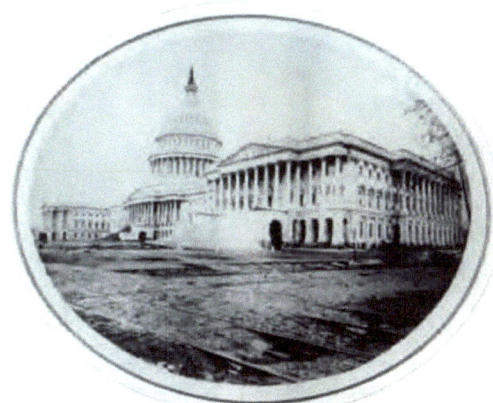

Fig. 9. U.S. Capitol, photographed according to Act of Congress, 1865. G. D. Wakely

drawn increasingly to contemporary European painting, which, at least in France, revolved around the artists who had become known as the impressionists. The impressionists' work was distinguished by a high-keyed palette and visible brushstrokes, giving the impression of a quick rendering, and often depicting subjects in motion or out-of-doors. Childe Hassam and William Merritt Chase introduced modified versions of the "new painting." A large number of American artists became more or less permanent expatriates. The cosmopolitan John Singer Sargent was drawn by a genuine love of Europe and also by the large number of wealthy patrons (see fig. 10). Culturally, Americans in general devoted themselves to European tastes and examples.

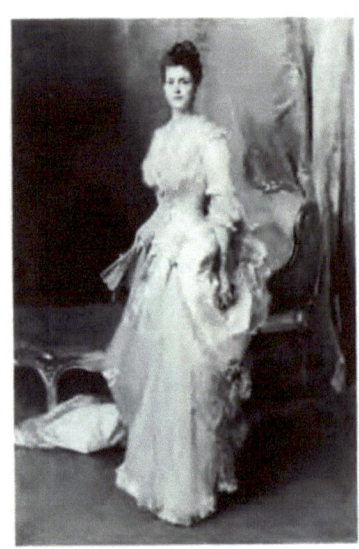

But for all the enthusiastic ostentation during the last quarter of the century, there was a widespread mood of unease and dissatisfaction in the country. The Gilded Age had its dark underside. Many Americans—certainly many artists—looked inward and meditated upon the related questions of the individual in American society and the regional and racial inequalities that still divided the nation. For example, the African-American painter Henry Ossawa Tanner (see slide 18) went to Europe primarily for reasons of racial and professional equality. Other factors, such as the enormous influx of immigrants and the attendant growth of cities and urban poverty, intensified the awareness of social and psychological conflicts. It is an ironic manifestation of the deep divisions and uncertainties of the era that only eight years after the Statue of Liberty was unveiled in 1886 ("Give me your tired, your poor, / Your huddled masses yearning to breathe free"), the Immigration Restriction League was formed.

American art and literature reflected this spiritual dichotomy, and the melancholy aura was evoked as often as the glittering surface of the age. Some artists, like John La Farge, turned to exotic lands and legends for their flights of fancy. Frederic Edwin Church traveled around South America, North Africa, the Mediterranean, and the Near East in search of grand themes that far surpassed the tourist views of lesser painters to suggest other worlds—of the mind no less than of geography. Still-life painters like William Harnett and John Frederick Peto created images that are musings on the irrevocability of time and life passed away (see fig. 11).

The paintings of Albert Pinkham Ryder and George Inness reflected the character of the artists as well as of the age. Ryder's oddly unreal pastures or ghostly moonlit paintings of boats in coves or tossed upon ominous, empty seas derive their haunting power from the

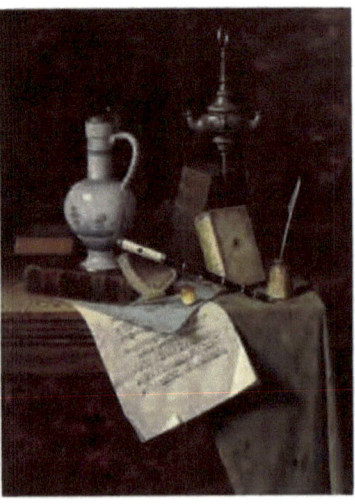

ABOVE: Fig. 10. John Singer Sargent, *Mrs. Henry White*, 1883, oil on canvas, The Corcoran Gallery of Art, Gift of the Honorable John Campbell White

Fig. 11. William M. Harnett, *My Gems*, 1888, oil on mahogany, National Gallery of Art, Washington, Gift of the Avalon Foundation

richness of Ryder's inner life—his imagination. More often he painted narrative pictures, though usually in landscape settings, and he was sometimes inspired by literature and music (see slide 13). In no sense an illustrator, Ryder found in the sister arts impulses to initiate his own pictorial inventions, reflecting his eccentric and excitable imagination. Since Inness was searching for an ideal, a spiritual unity, the actual landscape was often simply a point of departure. For example, although he painted many versions of Niagara Falls, the most famous of American natural wonders, only his first small painting was made at the falls. The rest were painted from memory, seemingly with little or no reference to his nature study. They became increasingly unrelated to topography, or even to the usual sensations of terror or awe at the falls, and turned rather into soft, diffuse fields of

Fig. 12 George Inness, *Sunset in the Woods*, 1891, oil on canvas. The Corcoran Gallery of Art, Museum Purchase

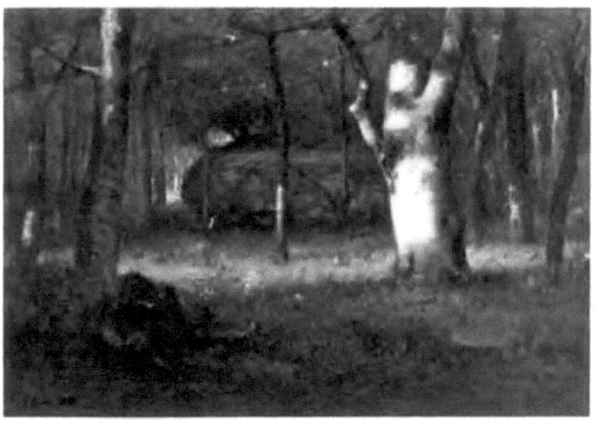

color that induce the viewer to meditate and contemplate the spiritual realities, what Inness called "the region of truth," that lie beyond the physical reality (see fig. 12).

The great artists of the century's end, Thomas Eakins and Winslow Homer, also expressed these darker forebodings. Eakins in many portraits delved into the spiritual unease of the time by adopting a somber palette reminiscent of Rembrandt and projecting onto his sitters his own brooding temperament (they were often displeased with the melancholy result). Although the probing realism that dominates American portraiture is still present, Eakins' paintings are often as much about reverie and reflection as they are about the sitter's features. Homer, for his part, had been a correspondent for *Harper's Weekly* for a short period during the Civil War, sending back drawings to be engraved for the journal. He thus had a first-hand experience of the atmosphere of the front lines, if not of the actual fighting, and he saw suffering and death among the Union soldiers, often from disease. Homer was a born observer, and his postwar paintings of wartime themes seem steeped in the conviction that responsibility for the catastrophe had to be impartially shared by all Americans, as the suffering had been, and as the healing would be. His paintings of the 1870s, in which scenes of rural America dominate, are about the land, the soil, and nature's regeneration.

It is significant that Homer habitually drew the horizon line high in his pictures throughout his career, placing his figures against a background of the earth—really *in* the earth rather than *on* it. Homer's landscapes are like no others in their combination of vivid, convincing description of what the artist saw and a primordial power that comes from his utter identification with nature. In their grandeur, his mature landscape and seascape paintings are the culmination of the native landscape tradition; alternately celebrating the beauty of America, proclaiming its potential, and offering critical reflections on the society that had settled it. Homer, however, went a step beyond even the pessimism of Thomas Cole to sound a resonant chord of fatalism. Nature was inherently heroic, but man was heroic only through stoicism.

Such an attitude seems startlingly modern, and it is. Homer's paintings summed up much of the nineteenth century, its beliefs and aspirations, yet many of them also announced a new century in which America's place was not yet certain. A democracy had survived a civil war, but its social fabric was torn in many places. Its economy had expanded astonishingly, but the center of its society had shifted from the country to the cities, where the disparity between rich and poor widened daily, and where the new Eden was nowhere to be found.

George Bellows was one of the young American artists who were grounded in the American artistic tradition of realism, and at the same time he was an exponent of the vigorous, expressionistic brushwork characteristic of modernist painting in the first decade of the twentieth century (see slide 20). In 1913 he was simultaneously elected a full member in the now-conservative National Academy of Design and included in the revolutionary Armory Show that jolted so many Americans into an awareness of modern art. Bellows embraced a subject that was not only contemporary but specifically urban: the American city in all its aspects, electric and gritty, teeming with people but unwelcoming. He understood the social displacements and struggles of the America he lived in as well as Winslow Homer had, but instead of Homer's fatalism he painted a vibrant, optimistic view of the outcome. With youthful heroism, together with other artists of his age, he welcomed the young century.

John Singleton Copley

John Singleton Copley (1738–1815)
Epes Sargent, **c. 1760 (pronounced "eps")**
Oil on canvas, 49⅞ x 40 in. (1.266 x 1.017 m)
National Gallery of Art, Gift of the Avalon
Foundation

Born in colonial Boston, Copley learned the rudiments of his art from his stepfather, an accomplished engraver but an only adequate painter. Copley learned what he could from engravings of English and European paintings, but he had few actual examples of fine painting in America from which to improve his technique. He felt "peculiarly unlucky in Liveing in a place into which there has not been one portrait brought that is worthy to be call'd a Picture within my memory" (see Charles Francis Adams, et al., ed., *Copley-Pelham Letters* [Boston, 1914]).

To make up for his lack of training, Copley scrutinized his subjects, delineating their shapes and their features through assiduous observation. The result was a detailed and realistic style that left no wrinkle and no double chin unrecorded. Such was Copley's genius as an observer that he described not only the appearance but also the character of his patrons. His career in the colonies lasted scarcely twenty years, for in 1774 he went to refine his art in Europe and never returned to the United States. But Cop-

ley completed several hundred memorable portraits of his contemporaries that guarantee his fame as the greatest American artist of that period.

Epes Sargent was a successful merchant, shipowner, landowner, and prominent citizen of Gloucester, Massachusetts. Sargent was about seventy when he was painted by Copley, who was in his early twenties. It is one of Copley's most imposing early portraits. Copley later painted portraits of Sargent's wife; his daughter and son-in-law; his son, Epes Sargent II, and daughter-in-law.

Sargent is shown standing in a casual yet dignified manner, leaning upon a column base set on a pedestal. The figure with a partial column was a traditional symbol of the virtue of fortitude, encompassing strength, courage, and endurance. The Roman column also points to Sargent's position as a pillar of the community and as the patriarch of his family.

The powerful physique of the elderly Sargent is accented by the remarkably heavy impasto (thickness of paint) on his face and especially on his hand—of which the painter Gilbert Stuart said, "Prick that hand and blood will spurt out" (see Augustus T. Perkins, *John Singleton Copley* [Boston, 1873]). Since the hand is placed at the very center of the painting, it is clear that Copley intended it to epitomize the forceful personality of his patron.

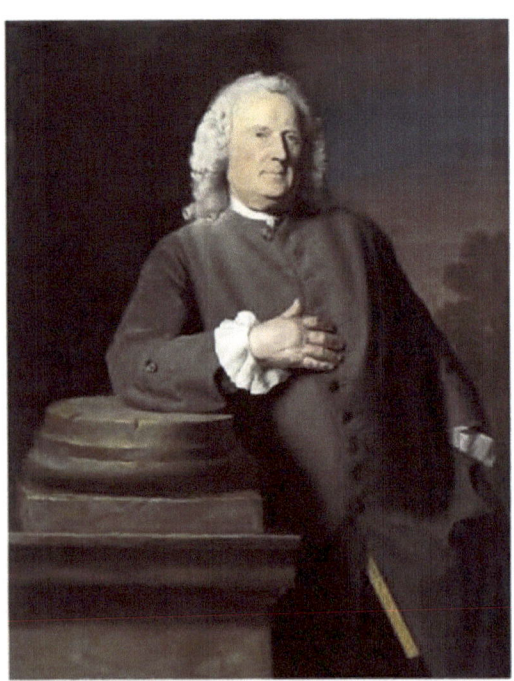

John Singleton Copley

John Singleton Copley (1738–1815)
Watson and the Shark, 1778
Oil on canvas, 71¼ x 90½ in. (1.821 x 2.297 m)
**National Gallery of Art, Ferdinand Lammot
Belin Fund**

When Copley embarked on his first trip to Europe in 1774, he had never included more than two figures in a painting. Even then he found it difficult to combine them with ease. He had no teacher and no paintings from which he could learn the techniques of perspective, fore-shortening, and modeling that made convincing multi-figure compositions possible. But once he had seen the narrative paintings of the Italian artists of the Renaissance and baroque, he quickly mastered the method and painted *Watson and the Shark*.

In this dramatic work Copley depicted ten figures as well as the shark and a harbor in the background. The subject was a recreation of an actual event, the rescue of Brook Watson from a shark attack in Havana Harbor in 1749. Ten years later Watson returned to his native England where he became a wealthy merchant. He had risen to become Lord Mayor of London when Copley met him and accepted his commission for this commemorative painting. The artist was able to put his newfound knowl-

edge of the art of the past to work. For instance, the two young men who strain to reach Watson are a quotation from a tapestry design by Raphael. For maximum emo-tional effect the figures are all placed in the foreground—at the front of the stage, as it were—where they are com-bined first into smaller groups that are then molded into a single unit shaped like a triangle or pyramid.

The extreme peril of the moment is even clearer when one realizes that the huge shark has already attacked once, and that Watson has lost part of his right leg below the knee (see the blood in the water). But in addition to the personal suffering of Watson, this painting may have rele-vance to the revolutionary war then in progress, for Wat-son was a leading Tory politician. While professing little sympathy for the rebel colonists, the Tories voiced loud opposition to slavery in America (the British offered free-dom for all African-Americans who joined the British army). The presence of the splendid black man, relatively calm and dignified at the apex of the pyramid, may refer to these abolitionist sentiments. If so, it is one of the earli-est artistic references to the evil of slavery in America. When Watson died, he specified in his will that this paint-ing be donated to an orphaned boys' school, "that it might serve a most usefull Lesson to Youth" (Public Record Office, London, 1805).

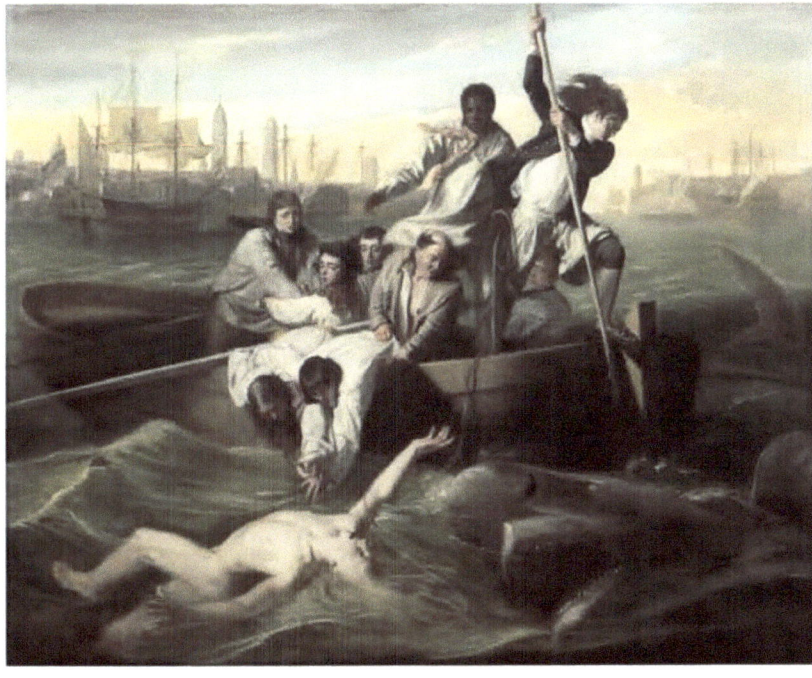

Gilbert Stuart

Gilbert Stuart (1755–1828)
Mrs. Richard Yates, 1793/1794
Oil on canvas, 30 x 25 in. (0.062 x 0.635 m)
National Gallery of Art, Andrew W. Mellon Collection

Mrs. Yates' long, bony face projects a shrewd, alert, and possibly peppery temperament, and Stuart's depiction of her as if interrupted in her sewing heightens this impression. "Get on with it," she seems to be thinking. "Can't you see I'm busy?" One wonders what she thought about Gilbert Stuart, who was known to entertain his sitters with witty conversation in order to keep their expressions lively.

Stuart was born in the colonies, but like John Singleton Copley, he went to England to establish himself in 1775. His prior training with an itinerant portrait painter was no match for artists schooled at the Royal Academy, however, and Stuart supported himself as a church organist. In desperation, he appealed to the American artist Benjamin West, who had a well-known studio in London: "att the age of 21 . . . [I] find myself Ignorant without Business or Freinds, without the necessarys of life so far that for some time I have been reduc'd to one miserable meal a day & frequently not even that" (see Richard

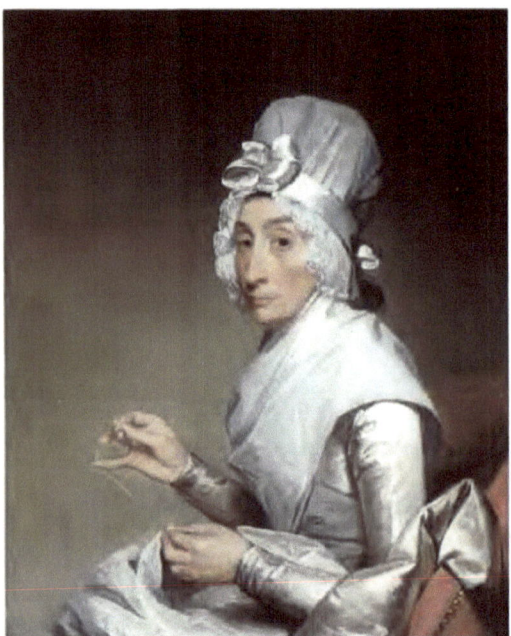

McLanathan, *Gilbert Stuart* [New York, 1986]). Stuart became West's protégé, studying with him for several years.

When Stuart returned to America in 1792, he was a highly successful artist with a more polished technique than any artist then painting here. He sought to secure his reputation as America's premier artist by painting George Washington, who finally sat for him in 1795. A prolific painter, Stuart produced numerous portraits not only of Washington but also of the following four presidents and many prominent citizens of the new United States. Mrs. Richard Yates was a New Yorker whose husband headed a prosperous import business. In the National Gallery's collection there are also individual portraits by Stuart of her husband, daughter, son-in-law, and brother-in-law.

Although wealthy, Mrs. Richard Yates wears a plain dress, her pompadoured hair concealed by a cap. She is placed asymmetrically against a neutral background that focuses attention on her figure so that her right hand is nearly as prominent as her face. It is this pose and the artist's superb drawing that are the key to the revelation of her personality. The precise outline of the figure, the wonderfully taut hand with needle, silver thimble, and thread, the crisply painted bonnet, and the clear bone structure of her face—all are achieved primarily through drawing with the brush. The silver-gray costume and the warm, translucent skin tones are painted in thin but subtly modulated layers of paint. The assured strokes of sparkling white highlighting her cap and dress suggest the spontaneity of the moment rather than the tiresome hours of sitting.

Stuart knew all the traditional poses and the European artistic custom of idealizing the men and women he painted—glossing over physical imperfections and generalizing personalities. Yet when he painted Mrs. Yates, he returned to the practice of colonial artists such as John Singleton Copley with a frank portrayal of character.

Rembrandt Peale

Rembrandt Peale (1787–1860)
Rubens Peale with a Geranium, 1801
Oil on canvas, 28⅛ x 24 in. (0.714 x 0.610 m)
National Gallery of Art, Patrons' Permanent Fund

This warm fraternal portrait glows with Rembrandt Peale's affection for his seventeen-year-old brother Rubens. The tenderness of the artist's conception, the quiet introspection of the sitter, and the emphasis on the intimate senses of sight, touch, and smell—all these factors join together to create a charming impression. Rembrandt and Rubens were part of the Peale clan, named by their father, Charles Willson Peale, after famous artists and scientists. Other siblings included Raphaelle, Titian, Angelica Kauffmann, Charles Linnaeus, and Benjamin Franklin Peale.

Rubens Peale had poor eyesight, indicated here by the two pairs of eyeglasses depicted, the second held in his left hand. The shadows and refracted gleam of the glasses he wears are painstakingly recorded, a mark of the family's love of science and invention. The Peale painters were well known for their fondness for illusionistic realism.

Charles Willson Peale had founded the nation's first systematic museum, which displayed portraits of leading citizens of the revolutionary war and federal eras together with natural history specimens such as the Chinese pheasants that Lafayette had sent to George Washington. Charles Willson Peale was a friend of Washington's and arranged on one occasion to have his sons Rembrandt and Raphaelle and his brother James join him when Washington sat for his portrait. Witnessing this, rival painter Gilbert Stuart remarked to Mrs. Washington that her husband was being "Pealed all round." Rembrandt Peale, in fact, established his reputation through his many portraits of George Washington that resulted from this single sitting, one of which is in the collection of the National Gallery of Art.

Rubens Peale, who eventually assumed management of the family museum, had a particular interest in botany.

I was very delicate in health and our family physician Dr. Hutchins required that I should be kept out of the sun. . . . I was not permitted to play in the streets with the other boys. . . . I made little progress in school for my sight was so imperfect.

One day when I returned from school I was informed that our family Physician was dead, at this intelligence I was so pleased that I danced about the room with joy, . . . and got to the shelf where my powders were kept and scraped them together and threw them into the fire. I then went into the garden and took the watering pot and watered my flowers which I was forbidden to do, and after that time I gradually increased in strength and health. ("Memorandum of Rubens Peale," Peale-Sellers Papers, American Philosophical Society, Philadelphia)

When Rubens had the opportunity to travel to England to exhibit his father's major discovery, a Mastodon skeleton, he was reluctant to leave his collection of rare plants in the care of others.

The geranium in its clay pot is as large and as lovingly painted as the young man who lays his hand on it so gently; the painting might equally be called "Portrait of a Geranium with Rubens Peale." Geraniums were extremely popular in Europe in the nineteenth century, proved by the many manuals on growing geraniums and the widespread belief in the geranium's medicinal uses. Thomas Jefferson himself had attempted unsuccessfully to grow geraniums in the United States. The prominence of the plant in this portrait is due to the family belief that it was the first geranium propagated in America.

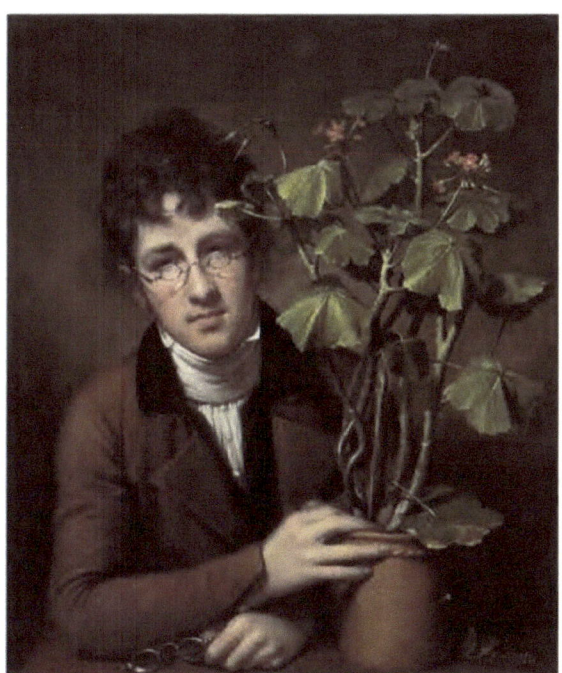

James Peale

James Peale (1749–1831)
Fruit Still Life with Chinese Export Basket, **1824**
Oil on panel, 14⅞ x 17¼ in. (0.378 x 0.456 m)
**National Gallery of Art, Gift of Mr. and Mrs. Thomas
M. Evans, in Honor of the Fiftieth Anniversary of
the National Gallery of Art**

Until the seventeenth century still-life painting was usually confined to details in paintings of other subjects or
decoration in domestic interiors. In seventeenth-century
Holland, however, still-life painting flourished and developed its own place in art. It became common also in nine-
teenth-century America, whose society was not unlike
that of earlier Holland: middle-class, mercantile, republican, mostly Protestant, and suffused with an ethos of
work, sobriety, and esteem for the realities of daily life.

Still-life painting in America was popularized largely
by various members of the Peale family. James Peale, a
brother of Charles Willson, painted miniatures until his
sight began to fail; he then turned to large-scale portraits,
landscapes, and still lifes. To avoid competing with his
nephew Raphaelle Peale, James did not exhibit any of his
still lifes until after Raphaelle's death in 1825. Raphaelle
had made still life his specialty, exhibiting as early as 1795
at the Columbianum Exhibition in Philadelphia, America's first public art exhibition. Although still-life painting
had a wide appeal, it was not highly valued. Raphaelle's
radiant still lifes typically sold for under forty dollars, in

comparison with Rembrandt's portraits and history scenes,
which fetched up to one hundred dollars.

Both James and Raphaelle followed a standard format
for their still lifes: a simple arrangement of fruits or veg-
etables with a few dishes or pieces of glassware, set on a
plain table or shelf before an unadorned, darkened wall.
The soft light unveils the glowing colors of the fruit. To an
extent, this format used by the Peales became the established representation of still life in American painting.

The Peale family's interest in botany has already been
noted in the discussion of the preceding painting by Rembrandt Peale. Like Rubens' geranium seen there, the fruit
in this still life has the appearance of being carefully, even
affectionately recorded. The dusty, translucent grapes, the
bruised and spotted apples, with the delicate but sturdy
porcelain basket as a foil for the fruit—all are successfully
realized. These effects are enhanced by contrasts, as for
instance the play of the round apples and grapes against
the darker, flatter leaves with serrate contours. James
Peale was unable to resist inventing one detail: the tendril
from the grape stem forms the artist's initials.

Perhaps because the artist was in his mid-seventies
when he painted this still life, the fruits in it have an
autumnal sense of ripeness and the beginnings of decay.
Grapes and apples both speak of harvest time, but their
isolation causes the viewer to look on them more closely,
with a thoughtful eye. Here, as in Dutch painting, the
blemished fruit clearly refers to the transience of life.

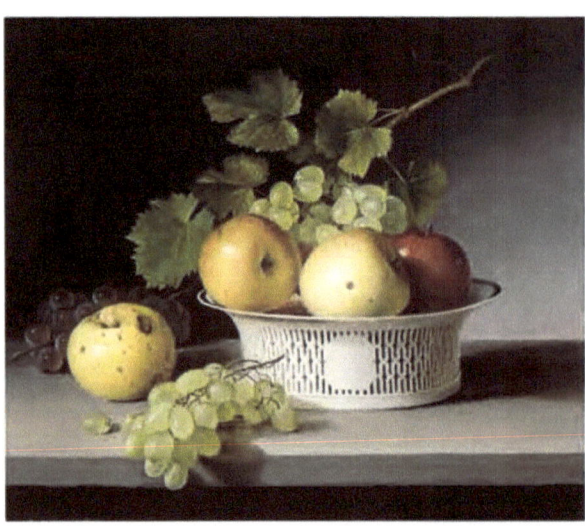

Joshua Johnson

Joshua Johnson (active 1796–1824)
The Westwood Children, c. 1807
Oil on canvas, 41⅛ x 46 in. (1.045 x 1.168 m)
National Gallery of Art, Gift of Edgar William and
Bernice Chrysler Garbisch

In 1798 Joshua Johnson described himself in an adver-
tisement in the *Baltimore Intelligence* as "a self-taught
genius, deriving from nature and industry his knowledge
of the art," who since he "experienced many insuperable
obstacles in the pursuit of his studies, it is highly gratify-
ing to him to make assurances of his ability to execute all
commands, with an effect, and in a style, which must give
satisfaction. . . ."

"Insuperable obstacles" was no exaggeration: Johnson
has the distinction of being the first professional black
artist in America. He is thought to have come to America
from the French West Indies. Johnson was probably a
household slave before purchasing his freedom through
his earnings from painting portraits. Very little is known
about his life, including the dates of his birth and death.
He most likely served in the household of a Baltimore
painter—perhaps Charles Peale Polk, a nephew of Charles
Willson Peale—and learned his craft from him. Johnson
used poses and props identical to those found in paintings
by Charles Peale Polk, especially during Johnson's early
period, before 1803. His connection with the Peales may
have secured his introduction to prosperous clientele.

Johnson was active as a portrait artist in Baltimore
between 1796 and 1824 and painted many prominent
residents of the city. Surviving are a considerable number
of portraits of children; to judge by his output, Johnson
was Baltimore's most popular painter of children.

Johnson's style is sometimes called "naive," referring
to a lack of formal art training, not to his character or ability. Naive artists usually have difficulty in suggesting
three-dimensional space convincingly, so interiors and figures look flat and abstract. But this "inability" is also the
source of the strengths in naive art: pattern and silhouette
as well as emotional directness. Johnson's figures are stiff,
yet the stares of the three boys fix the viewer's attention.
The reason is related to the focused intensity with which
Johnson himself looked at these children and their bird
dog. He liked to vary his compositions, here by introduc-
ing a receding wall and a view through a window. But the
illusion of recession is slight and one is struck instead by
the artist's strong sense of flat design—the shapes of the
figures and the sparely painted planes of walls and floors.

As is characteristic of Johnson, his color relationships
are beautiful and subtle, evidenced by the hunter green
costumes against the thinly painted purplish-blue wall.
Bands of color are also used to tie the composition together: the white ruffled collars, the black boots and dog, and
the red cherries and roses. At first, the boys do not seem
very individual, but a closer look reveals aspects of their
varying ages and personalities. The child on the right,
John, is about nine years old and displays the greatest
assurance. His hand rests on the shoulder of the youngest
child, named George Washington, who at age three, has
the most open expression. The boy on the left, Henry, is
probably five or six, and his face conveys a slight timidity.
Each boy holds attributes: a sprig of cherries and roses.
Both the fresh fruit and the cut flowers are traditionally
associated with fragility and youthful charm, while the
dog with the captured bird may allude to the freedom and
fleeting innocence of childhood.

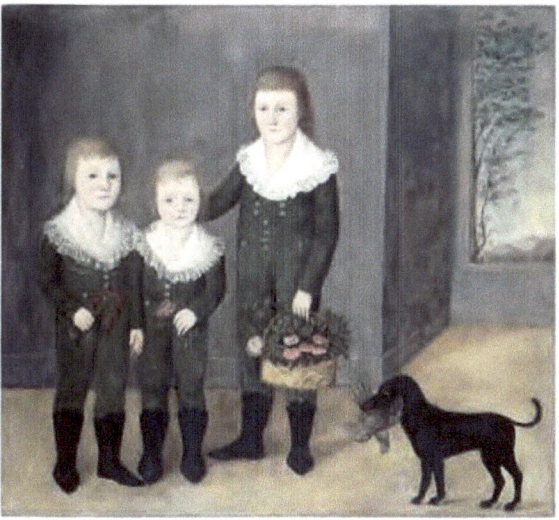

Edward Hicks

Edward Hicks (1780–1849)
Peaceable Kingdom, c. 1834
Oil on canvas, 29⅛ x 35½ in. (0.745 x 0.901 m)
National Gallery of Art, Gift of Edgar William and Bernice Chrysler Garbisch

Edward Hicks is probably the most celebrated American naive or "folk" painter. He made his living as a painter of coaches and signs, but he had no professional training. As was common for artists of the nineteenth century, Hicks borrowed many of his figures and motifs from popular engravings. His best-known subject is the *Peaceable King-dom*, of which he painted at least sixty versions. He began this series in his forties and continued it until the end of his life.

The painting actually has two different scenes. The first is in the foreground, where there is a crowd of large and small animals and three small children. It is a charmingly literal interpretation of a poem from the Old Testament (Isaiah 11:6–7) prophesying:

> The wolf also shall dwell with the lamb,
> and the leopard shall lie down with the kid;
> and the calf and the young lion and the fatling together;
> and a little child shall lead them.
> And the cow and the bear shall feed;
> their young ones shall lie down together;
> and the lion shall eat straw like the ox.

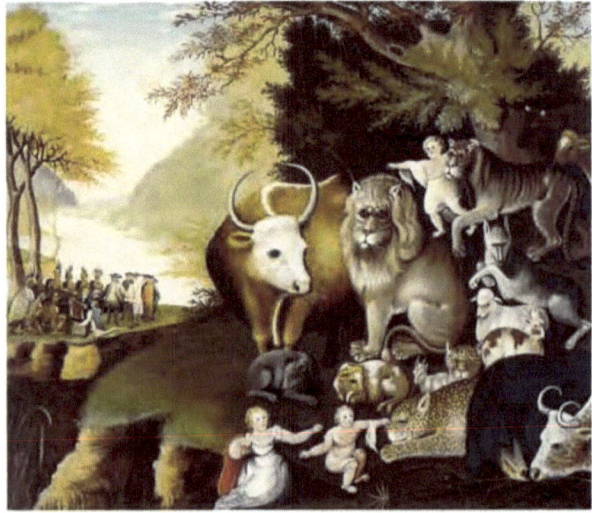

The passage ends with "They shall not hurt or destroy in all my holy mountain: for the earth shall be full of the knowledge of the Lord, as the waters cover the sea."

In the background small figures act out the historical event in which William Penn signed a land and peace treaty with the Lenape Indians. In another painting of this treaty in the National Gallery, Hicks inscribed: "PENNS Treaty with the INDIANS, made 1681 with out an Oath and never broken. The Foundation of Religious and Civil LIBERTY, in the U.S. of AMERICA." William Penn was a Quaker, a member of a religious sect that was persecuted in England. Penn persuaded King Charles II to permit Quakers to colonize the land later called "Penn's Woods" or Pennsylvania. Penn was known for his integrity and just dealings, and the Lenape and English colonists lived in unusual harmony.

Both scenes symbolize the ideal of peace on earth and match the Quaker vision of utopia, a search for unity between humanity and God. Hicks had been a Quaker minister since 1811, an unpaid and itinerant career. His cousin Elias Hicks was also a Quaker preacher, and famous among country Quakers for his fiery sermons. Elias Hicks emphasized the mystical aspect of submission to the Inner Light. In 1827 Elias led the separation between the traditional rural Quakers, who opposed the urban members' emphasis on scripture over revelation. Edward Hicks, although supporting his cousin's position, urged the healing of this schism among the Quakers. Certainly his *Peaceable Kingdom* paintings are an allegory for the conciliation of adversaries.

As a young man Hicks had been a hard drinker and had led a wild life given over to "the strength of my passions" (Edward Hicks, *Memoirs of the Life and Religious Labors of Edward Hicks* [Philadelphia, 1851]). When he reformed, he suffered the Quakers' disapproval of painting, which he himself considered "the inseparable companion of voluptuousness and pride." He therefore gave his paintings to friends rather than sell them. His doubts about his own spiritual worth seem to be expressed in the uneasy eyes of some of his animals. As historian James Thomas Flexner wrote, Hicks, confronted with his own temptations, "knew that the lion would not find it easy to lie down with the lamb" (see Flexner 1969 [vol. 3, 1954]).

Thomas Cole

Thomas Cole (1801–1848)
The Notch of the White Mountains (Crawford Notch), 1839
Oil on canvas, 40 x 61½ in. (1.016 x 1.560 m)
National Gallery of Art, Andrew W. Mellon Fund

This autumnal landscape holds the modern viewer spellbound in admiration of the natural beauty of New England, reinforced by nostalgia for a supposedly simpler age. Thomas Cole was one of the founders of the Hudson River School of painting. He was keenly aware of "the want of associations such as arise amid scenes of the old world" (Thomas Cole, "Lecture on American Landscape Delivered before the Catskill Lyceum," *Northern Light* 1 [1841]), and he believed that the land, rather than a common history or culture, was America's distinction and heritage. For Cole and his contemporaries the landscape, while appreciated for its beauty, often had a more complex and profound meaning.

The fall season is a traditional symbol of the passage of human life, particularly the onset of old age. That meaning is emphasized here by the stumps and dead trees in the foreground (on one of which Cole has, significantly, inscribed his name). The ancient gnarled tree is a typical device used by Cole to underscore the venerableness of America's wilderness. A sense of ominousness is conveyed by the dark shadow of an approaching storm. The horseman and the tiny figures standing before the house to greet him seem engulfed by the immense scale of their surroundings.

This painting actually refers to a specific event. In August 1826 a tremendous avalanche at Crawford Notch took the lives of the Willey family, nine in all. Crawford Notch is in the White Mountains of New Hampshire and is a well-known scenic site; Cole himself had been to the Notch several times. In 1828 he wrote in his diary: "We now entered the Notch, and felt awestruck as we passed between the bare and rifted mountains. . . . The sight of the Willey House, with its little patch of green in the gloomy desolation, very naturally recalled to mind the horror of the night when the whole family perished beneath an avalanche of rocks and earth" (see L. L. Noble, *The Life and Works of Thomas Cole* [Cambridge, MA, 1964]).

It is not surprising that Cole, by nature a pessimist and steeped in literature, would use this sad event to add meaning to a landscape painting. Virtually everyone would connect this painting to the avalanche, for the tragedy was widely publicized. It also inspired Nathaniel Hawthorne to write a short story, "The Ambitious Guest," published in *Twice-Told Tales* in 1837, only two years before Cole's painting. Hawthorne wrote: "Who has not heard their name? The story has been told far and wide, and will forever be a legend of these mountains. Poets have sung their fate." By choosing to depict the site, rather than the event, Cole instills the landscape with symbolic significance. As Hawthorne wrote in his story: "The simplest words must intimate, but not portray, the unutterable horror of the catastrophe."

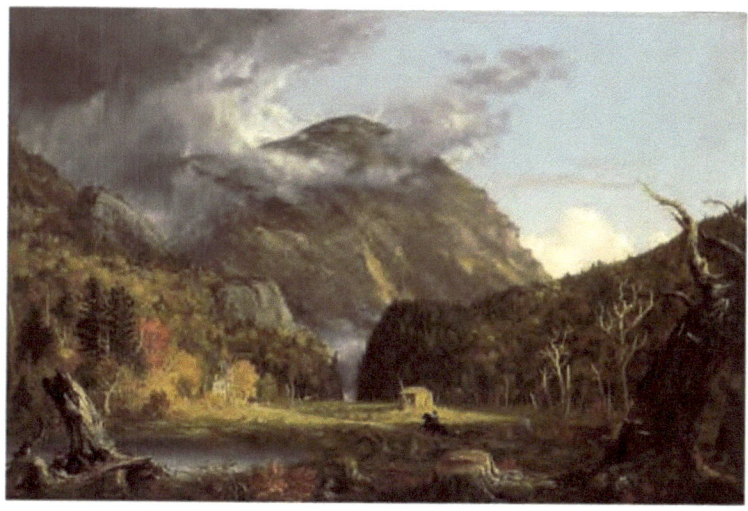

John Quidor

John Quidor (1801–1881)
The Return of Rip Van Winkle, c. 1849
Oil on canvas, 39¼ x 49¼ in. (1.010 x 1.265 m)
National Gallery of Art, Andrew W. Mellon
Collection

American art and literature grew up together. Some artists, including John Quidor, chose to represent and interpret scenes from novels and short stories. Quidor was especially attracted to the works of Fenimore Cooper and Washington Irving, America's most famous fiction writers in the first half of the nineteenth century; their prose evoked the still-exotic wilderness of America and the imaginative and fantastic legends spawned by the New World. No other painter so effectively translated the ironic and dramatic literary inventions of Irving as did Quidor, whose quirky, idiosyncratic painting style proved a perfect match for Irving's prose in "Rip Van Winkle" from *The Sketch Book* (1819).

After his twenty-year sleep in the Catskills, Rip has unknowingly returned to a postrevolutionary America—on election day. Quidor follows Irving's description precisely, from the "large rickety wooden building . . . over the door [of which] was painted, 'The Union Hotel, by Jonathan Doolittle,'" to the "flag, on which was a singular assemblage of stars and stripes," and the sign where in place of the face of King George was a head "decorated with a cocked hat, and underneath was painted in large characters, GENERAL WASHINGTON."

Quidor is just as faithful to Irving's description of Rip, "with his long, grizzled beard, his rusty fowling-piece, his uncouth dress." He includes Rip's son and namesake leaning against the tree, "apparently as lazy, and certainly as ragged" as he himself had been twenty years before, and the "knowing, self-important old gentleman, in a sharp cocked hat," who asks Rip who he is. "God knows, exclaimed [Rip], at his wit's end; I'm not myself—I'm somebody else—that's me yonder—no—that's somebody else got into my shoes—I was myself last night, but I fell asleep on the mountain, and they've changed my gun, and everything's changed, and I'm changed, and I can't tell what's my name, or who I am!" Quidor shows Rip as an embattled but defiant figure.

The implications of Quidor's painting go beyond a literal reading of the story line. This picture may also convey the identity crisis of a new nation, a people who do not yet know who they are and who find themselves in changed circumstances. Quidor paints a baby climbing the flagpole of the recently born stars and stripes, and he places the elderly Rip before a house built in the Dutch style, a relic from the days of the Dutch colonization of New York.

Quidor may also have identified himself with the isolated Rip Van Winkle, for Quidor is unique in his style, an anachronism in American art, and out of step with the mainstream. Quidor was a painter of signs and banners for the New York fire departments; his hopes for the success of his large history and religious paintings were never realized, although he was not unpopular. This painting's success results from Quidor's clear organization of figures and above all from the strong rhythms of angles and curves and the animated brushwork that matches the vigor of Irving's vivid prose.

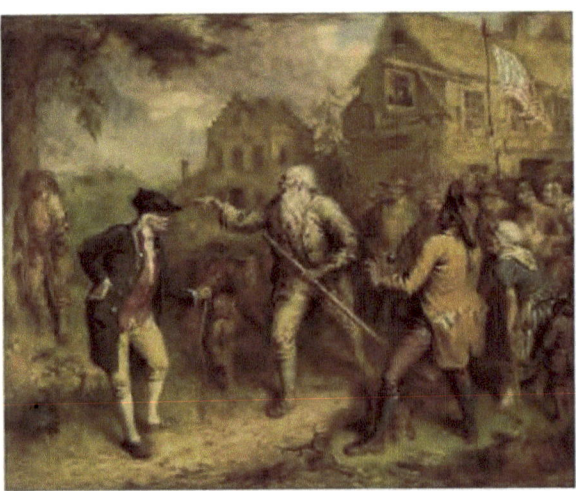

George Inness

George Inness (1825–1894)
The Lackawanna Valley, 1855
Oil on canvas, 33⅞ x 50¼ in. (0.860 x 1.275 m)
National Gallery of Art, Gift of Mrs. Huttleston Rogers

As a young artist, just returned from travel and study abroad and temporarily without money, Inness could not refuse the commission for this painting, though it paid him only seventy-five dollars. It was ordered for advertising purposes by the president of the new Delaware, Lackawanna & Western Rail Road, who directed him to include four trains and a roundhouse at Scranton, Pennsylvania. The D. L. & W. R. R. Company was dissatisfied with *The Lackawanna Valley*, however, and demanded that Inness put the initials of the railroad on at least one engine. At his wife's urging, Inness complied. In 1891, when Inness was a famous artist, he found this picture for sale in a curiosity shop in Mexico City and was able to buy it back for fifty dollars.

The requisite railway equipment is centrally placed in this composition, but it is settled into the panoramic landscape. Inness balances the steam that rises from behind the roundhouse with another plume of smoke at the left center, but he silhouettes a church steeple against the smoke, obscuring its industrial source. Church and roundhouse, both man-made, are balanced, almost paired. The engine that determinedly pulls a line of coal cars toward the foreground seems remarkably unintrusive in the vast sweep of the landscape—no iron monster, this. Human intervention is also apparent in the foreground, which is cleared of all its trees save one. Yet this towering tree dominates the painting, as much by its expressive grace and beauty as by its size. It unites the receding planes of the landscape, and together with the reclining boy, who (like the artist or the viewer) gazes quietly into this New World landscape, it helps to resolve this painted meditation on the relationship between humanity and nature.

Although Inness was not opposed to progress as exemplified by the railroad, the commission provided an opportunity for him to comment on the convergence of human intervention and divine creation. In his late works Inness can be described as a painter of the landscapes of memory. He revered the land as the embodiment of divine essence. His religious mysticism was an extension of the New England transcendentalism of Emerson and others. Inness wanted the viewer to feel in front of his paintings as the actress Fanny Kemble had once felt in front of nature: "carried into the immediate presence of God" (see O'Brien 1981).

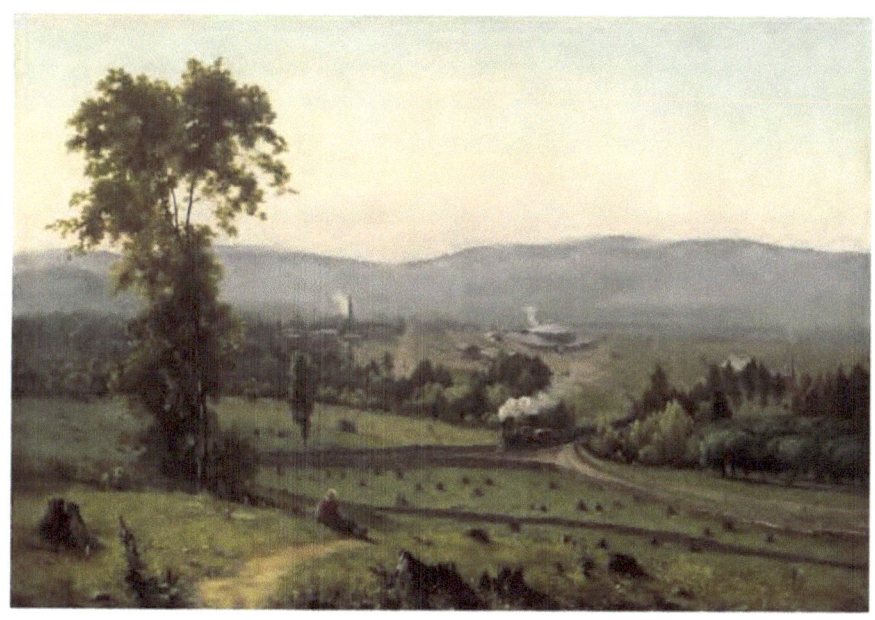

John Frederick Kensett

John Frederick Kensett (1816–1872)
Beacon Rock, Newport Harbor, **1857**
Oil on canvas, 22½ x 36 in. (0.572 x 0.914 m)
National Gallery of Art, Gift of Frederick Sturges, Jr.

Most of Kensett's paintings of rivers, lakes, or coastline, like this one, are characterized by an almost motionless serenity and by a bold simplicity of design that seems to predict some of the abstract paintings of the twentieth century. Many of his landscapes are entirely without or almost without human beings. In *Beacon Rock,* for instance, only a lone fisherman and the implied presence of sailors in the few distant sailboats are introduced—and absorbed—into the scene.

The painting seems extremely minimal at first glance. A fort is shown in the left distance, and one can barely detect its red flag. Several sailboats and a narrow band of land interrupt the smooth horizon. The most prominent feature of the painting is the headland of Beacon Rock thrusting into the water from the right. This rock is the most active element in the painting, not only for its size but for its irregular contour and variegated surface.

Kensett regulates the transition from foreground to the far distance by marking the spatial recession with these few elements: shore, rock, fort, and sailboats. He manages to keep the massive rock in its place by allowing the blue-green "ground" layer of paint to show through the thinly painted ochres of the rock mass. This fuses the different parts into a single unit, with no disruptions of either the spatial or surface unity of the painting.

Kensett painted scenes of Newport Harbor, Rhode Island, a number of times, with each view exhibiting subtle shifts in light, placement, and perspective. He worked as an engraver of banknotes before becoming a full-time painter in the 1840s, and the immaculate detail and precision of his landscapes seem due in part to his early training. Kensett was one of the Hudson River School of landscape painters; like Thomas Cole, he depicted the New Hampshire White Mountains. But whereas Cole used landscape in *The Notch of the White Mountains* to convey a sense of foreboding, Kensett creates a scene of tranquility through his lucid, even light and ordered nature. This quietude contrasts with the turbulence of the Civil War period, and the public yearned for and delighted in such scenes of peaceful calm. Eminently respected during his lifetime, Kensett was a founder of the Metropolitan Museum of Art in 1870.

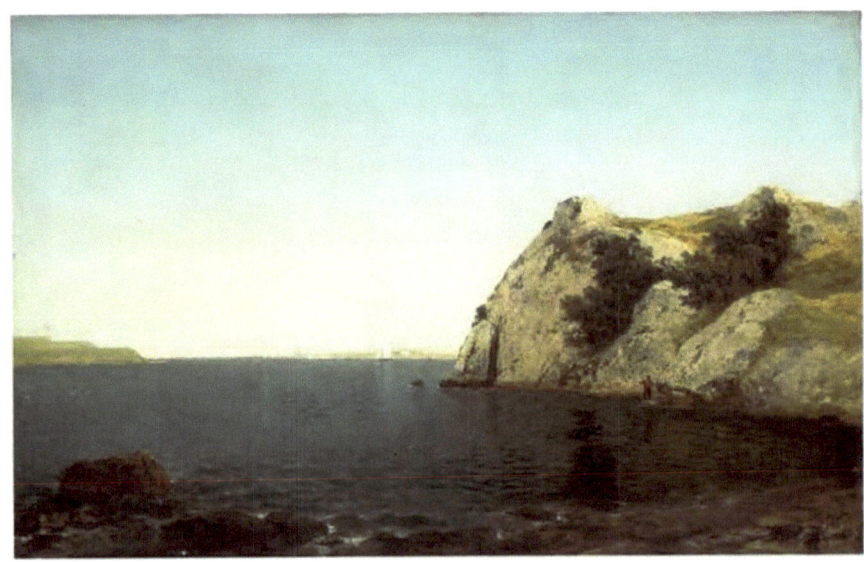

Frederic Edwin Church

Frederic Edwin Church (1826–1900)
Morning in the Tropics, 1877
Oil on canvas, 54⅛ x 84⅛ in. (1.381 x 2.137 m)
National Gallery of Art, Gift of the Avalon
Foundation

Frederic Edwin Church was the leading Hudson River School painter. Like Thomas Cole, his teacher, Church was an artist who saw the landscape as a symbol of the divine. Cole and Church shared the prevailing view of the American continent as a new Eden, where mankind could seek a fresh spiritual beginning. Church specialized in the expansive, epic landscape paintings that were adored by the American public until the close of the century.

The artist suffered from crippling rheumatism that shortened his career, and *Morning in the Tropics* is his last major painting. It is also a radiant statement of his religious faith. Cole had once used tropical foliage as a symbol of the infancy of mankind in a specifically Christian sense. Church actually traveled to South America and painted the lush tropical landscape often and with a passion that was essentially religious. He seemed to see the volcanoes and the great rivers of the "New World" as metaphors for both life's beginning and its end.

In 1880 Church exhibited this painting with the title *The River of Light,* which suggests its metaphysical significance for him. It was an appropriate title, for the whole of the large picture is suffused with light. The sun is partially obscured, and its light is actually brighter in its reflection in the water. This painting is a cosmic image that embodies Church's belief in the omnipresence of God throughout creation. Following the flight of the birds into the distance, where the stream disappears into the luminous mists, is a tiny boat with a single figure. The voyager is very possibly a symbol of the soul entering paradise.

At Church's death, his friend Charles Dudley Warner wrote, "We can scarcely overestimate the debt of America to Mr. Church in teaching it to appreciate the grandeur and beauty of its own scenery, and by his work at home and in tropical lands in inculcating a taste and arousing an enthusiasm for landscape art—that is, landscape art as an expression of the majesty and beauty of the divine" (see Franklin Kelly, *Frederic Edwin Church* [Washington, D.C., 1989]).

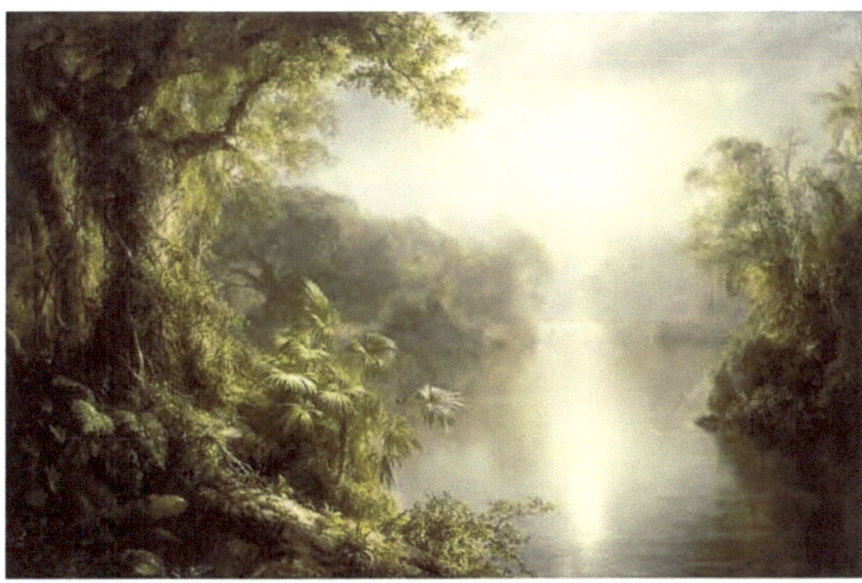

Albert Pinkham Ryder

Albert Pinkham Ryder (1847–1917)
Siegfried and the Rhine Maidens, 1888/1891
Oil on canvas, 19⅞ x 20½ in. (0.505 x 0.520 m)
National Gallery of Art, Andrew W. Mellon
Collection

Ryder is known as the visionary of American art. He had little formal education or professional training in painting. Instead, Ryder lived a rich life of the imagination, producing surreal and magical paintings.

Richard Wagner's opera *Die Gotterdammerung* ("The Twilight of the Gods"), the last opera in his Ring cycle, was produced at the Metropolitan Opera in 1888. The moment Ryder chose for this painting is from act 3, scene 1, of the opera, when the hero, Siegfried, encounters the Rhine maidens, who demand the return of a ring made of the Rhine gold stolen from them (in the first opera of the cycle). The "bewitching" and "sensuous" music of this scene had made a great impression on audiences and, obviously, on Ryder.

Ryder remembered, "I had been to hear the opera and went home about twelve o'clock and began this picture. I worked for forty-eight hours without sleep or food, and the picture was the result" (see Kathleen Preciado, ed., *Albert Pinkham Ryder* [Washington, D.C., 1989]). In spite of this remark, the technical evidence of the painting itself shows it to have been worked on for a longer period, and it was not exhibited until 1891. It was typical of Ryder to keep pictures in his studio for a long time, reworking them and often building up thick and complex paint layers that dazzled the eyes. Ryder was known for preparing and experimenting with various, and often unstable, combinations of pigment, wax, ashes, varnish, and alcohol to create the desired paint quality.

The details of Wagner's music drama are not necessary to know, for Ryder did not illustrate the music or the drama so much as create a visual equivalent that has its own mysterious life. The shapes and gestures of the Rhine maidens and Siegfried are echoed and magnified by the violently swaying, undulating trees and have powerful rhythms like those of music. Here the eerie, almost supernatural colors of moonlight are as evocative as the musical harmonies of Wagner. Ryder loved moonlight; he often walked the streets of New York at night. Ryder's most famous paintings are of sailing boats illuminated by pale moonlight.

The dark, inward-turning nature of the painting is also a characteristic to be found in many other American works of art toward the end of the nineteenth century, reflecting a lingering somberness from the Civil War era. The energy here is expressed as spiritual turmoil, and the artist paints an imaginary, not a real world.

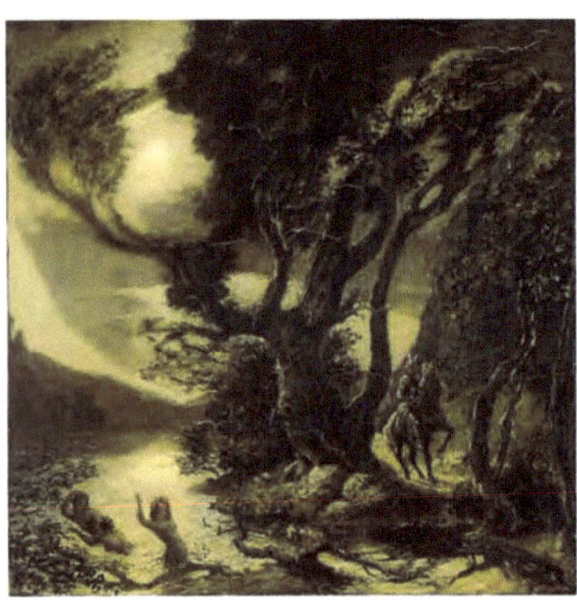

Winslow Homer

Winslow Homer (1836–1910)
Breezing Up (A Fair Wind), 1876
Oil on canvas, 24⅛ x 38⅛ in. (0.615 x 0.970 m)
National Gallery of Art, Gift of the W. L. and
May T. Mellon Foundation

This image of youthful freedom has a deeper meaning and resonance when one considers that it was finished in the year of the nation's centennial celebration, with the horror of the recent Civil War still hovering in everyone's mind. The innocence of childhood was a popular postwar theme as the country tried to regain its revolutionary optimism. The original title of the painting, *A Fair Wind*, fits the determinedly hopeful mood of the period.

Homer had been a Civil War correspondent, providing drawings for illustrations in *Harper's Weekly*. For more than a decade after the war he turned mostly to rural America for his subjects. Both the peacefulness of these scenes and their restrained nostalgia for the prewar era struck a responsive chord in Americans, and many of Homer's paintings of this period, including this one, were reproduced as magazine illustrations.

This enchanting, light-flooded painting, with its dynamic brushwork and tangible immediacy, is at the same time curiously aloof and controlled. The boat's motion is reinforced by the large sailboat on a parallel course to the right. Yet it is also slowed by the merging of the sail with the edge of the canvas. Although the viewers are brought close to the boat—as if we were also sailing—the man and three boys do not notice us. And although they are indeed involved with handling the boat, they seem more thoughtful than active, preoccupied with something inside themselves or outside the scene. The ambiguity of Homer's paintings is described by one critic who wrote in 1878 that "Mr. Homer . . . paints his own thoughts—not other persons' " (see Lloyd Goodrich, *Winslow Homer* [New York, 1945]).

That Homer intended his picture to suggest meanings beyond the simple description of an everyday activity is likely, for he worked on this painting on and off for three years. Interestingly, one of the changes that he made during this long process is noticeable: just to the right of the boat one can faintly see the shapes of the sails of a boat that he later decided to eliminate. Such a reappearance—due to chemical changes and surface wear—of an over-painted area is known as a *pentimento* (literally, in Italian, "repentance").

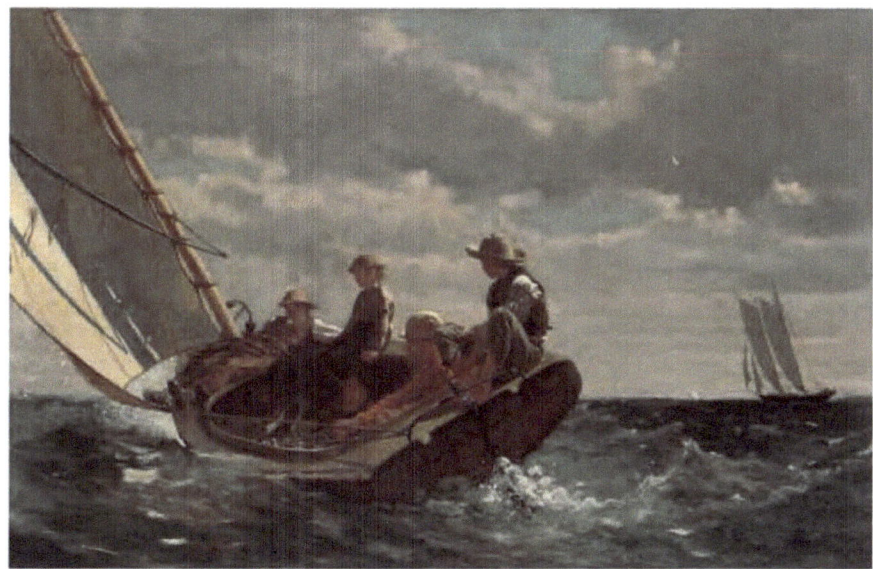

Thomas Eakins

Thomas Eakins (1844–1916)
The Biglin Brothers Racing, c. 1873
Oil on canvas, 24⅛ x 36⅛ in. (0.612 x 0.916 m)
National Gallery of Art, Gift of Cornelius Vanderbilt Whitney

Thomas Eakins received most of his artistic training during four years' study in Paris, at exactly the time when the impressionists began asserting their independence from the conservative, academic painting of the French art world. The impressionists were united in a desire to paint scenes from modern life rather than the traditional narrative subjects that had dominated Western art since the Renaissance. In addition, they often painted out-of-doors so that they could capture the colors and quickly changing effects of natural light.

Apparently Eakins, whose teacher was one of the academics disliked by the impressionists, never saw the new painting when he was in Paris. But he did share the impressionists' passion for recording modern life, demonstrated by a series of rowing pictures he painted from 1870 until 1875. Although the brightness of the light gleaming on the scullers' shirts and paddle in this painting is striking, Eakins contrasts it with dark shadows, and the painting as a whole has a dark tonality.

Unlike the impressionists, Eakins painted in the studio and was always more interested in volumetric form than insubstantial atmosphere. His concern with achieving the illusion of solid objects convincingly placed in the picture space led him to make elaborate perspective drawings for his paintings of champion racers sculling. This also had the effect, as he must have realized, of suspending the sense of movement—for a one-point perspective system is by nature static. The effect of a stop-motion photograph is increased by cropping both ends of the scull, locking it in place. That this was intentional becomes clear when one knows that the first title of the painting was *The Biglin Brothers About to Start the Race*—the movement is yet to come!

Recreational and sporting activities on the Delaware or Schuylkill Rivers were favorite summer pastimes in Philadelphia. The figure in motion—particularly the rhythmic, repeated motion required by sculling—interested Eakins, especially at this time when he was studying anatomy at Jefferson Medical College. Eakins continued throughout his career to investigate human anatomy and movement; when he was an instructor at the Pennsylvania Academy of the Fine Arts, his insistence on using nude male models, even for coed classes, instigated a controversy that led to his resignation in 1886. Eakins followed in the tradition of realism, and his highly developed skills of observation and study go far to make him one of America's greatest artists.

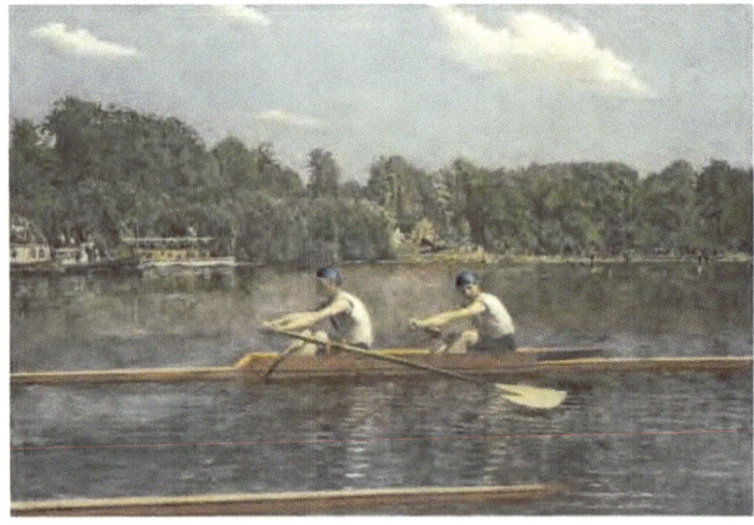

James McNeill Whistler

James McNeill Whistler (1834–1903)
The White Girl (Symphony in White, No. 1), **1862**
Oil on canvas, 84½ x 42½ in. (2.147 x 1.080 m)
National Gallery of Art, Harris Whittemore Collection

James McNeill Whistler was a leading figure in the French avant-garde. Born in Lowell, Massachusetts, he spent his entire adult life as an expatriate, mostly in London and Paris, and his art has a European urbanity and self-conscious aestheticism. It had no counterpart in American painting until near the end of the century, when his art became an important influence in the United States.

The White Girl became internationally notorious when it was rejected by exhibitors in both London and Paris. Its strange mixture of flatness with three-dimensionality and coolness with aggressiveness made the painting controversial from the start. The white on white of gown against draperies is elegant but recessive and flat (the flatness is emphasized by the signature at the top right, which ignores the pleats in the draperies). The scumbled paint and individual brushstrokes also serve to bring attention to the flat surface of the picture plane. Such explicit flatness, which proclaims the two-dimensional nature of painting, was a very recent concept in art, and the subtle artifice of the restricted palette was equally daring.

Whistler's model, Joanna Heffernan, was also his mistress, yet he clearly relates the color white to purity and the lily she holds to virginity. Her head is set off by a mass of dark red hair. The bear rug over the flowered carpet is startling. Most of it tilts up toward the picture plane, not suggesting depth, but the bear's head is strongly modeled and sharply foreshortened; it seems alive and menacing, especially since it is near the viewer's eye level. There may have been a private reference to the intimate relationship between painter and model, but in any case, the contrast between her impassive face and the fierce bear's head at her feet is emotionally charged.

Although the subtitle *Symphony in White, No. 1*, was added six years after *The White Girl* was painted, it was among the first works in which the painting itself, not just its subject, was important. Whistler was interested in finding equations between music and painting. "Why should not I call my works 'symphonies,' 'arrangements,' 'harmonies,' and 'nocturnes'?" he wrote. "As music is the poetry of sound, so is painting the poetry of sight, and the subject-matter has nothing to do with harmony of sound or of color" (James McNeill Whistler, *The Gentle Art of Making Enemies* [London, 1890]). Twenty-five years later Whistler would fully develop the theory of "art for art's sake" that became the cornerstone of modern art.

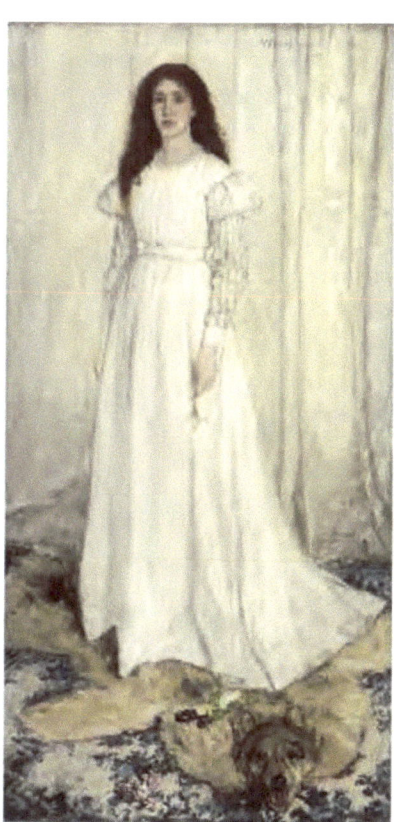

William Merritt Chase

William Merritt Chase (1849–1916)
A Friendly Call, 1895
Oil on canvas, 30⅛ x 48¼ in. (0.765 x 1.225 m)
National Gallery of Art, Chester Dale Collection

The interior of Chase's studio at Shinnecock, Long Island, was the setting for this elegant, intimate, delicious scene. This studio, like Chase's Tenth Street Studio in Manhattan, was, according to a contemporary, "the sanctum sanctorum of the aesthetic fraternity," who gathered there "midst painting, statuary, music, flowers, and flamingos (stuffed)" (see *William Merritt Chase* [Santa Barbara, 1964]). This refined ambience was self-conscious and reminiscent of Whistler, whom Chase had known since 1885. Chase's taste was genuinely international. He once remarked, "My God, I'd rather to Europe than go to heaven" (W. J. Williams, *A Heritage of American Painting from the National Gallery of Art* [Maplewood, NJ, 1981]).

Prints, paintings, and textiles cover the wall or are reflected in the large mirror. Also reflected are the door and windows, the source of the light that suffuses the room. Together with the cushions on the settee, these objects are ingeniously arranged as a complex series of rectangles within rectangles, all contained within the unusually low, wide rectangle of the painting itself.

The irregular contours of the two women soften the rectilinear formality of the design. The figures merge with their comfortable surroundings, since the white and pale yellow costumes blend with other light colors in the room. For Chase the subject of the women's conversation appears to be art itself, for he has cleverly placed them on either side of the center space so that they face each other across two framed works of art.

Inspiration for the fascinating composition may have come from the great Spanish painter Velázquez, or another seventeenth-century artist, the Dutch painter Vermeer, who was rediscovered in the late nineteenth century. Both Velázquez and Vermeer painted women in light-filled interiors and used the device of the mirror to reveal the opposite side of the room. In addition, the great French impressionist Edgar Degas, Chase's contemporary, painted very similar compositions. Chase, as an American impressionist, certainly adopted French impressionism's high-keyed color. *A Friendly Call* is, in every aspect, a quiet celebration of art and artists.

At his summer art school at Shinnecock as well as in New York, Chase taught a generation of artists. As teacher and painter, he brought the American landscape tradition into the twentieth century. Chase's students, among them Georgia O'Keeffe and Edward Hopper, benefited both from his instruction and his example.

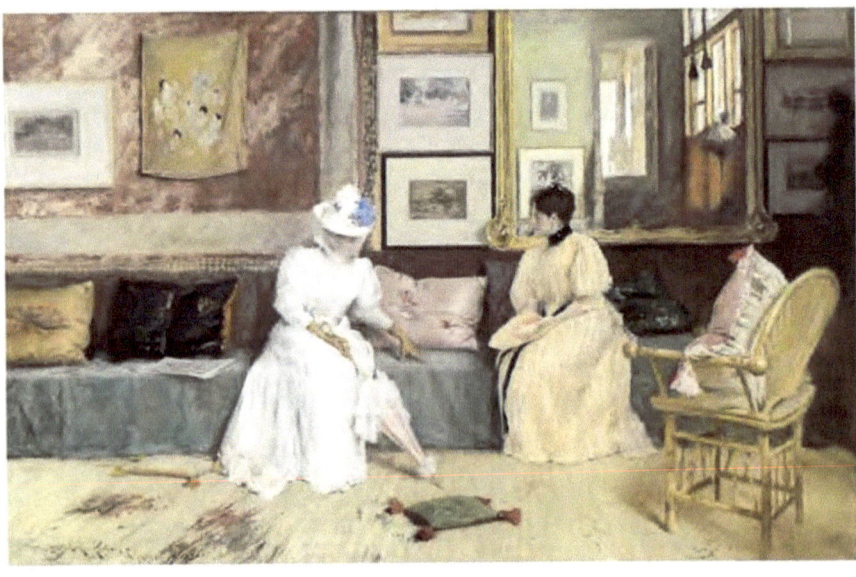

Henry Ossawa Tanner

Henry Ossawa Tanner (1859–1937)
The Seine, **1902**
Oil on canvas, 9 x 13 in. (0.230 x 0.329 m)
National Gallery of Art, Gift of the Avalon
Foundation

Tanner loved France as much as Chase or Whistler did, but his motivation was quite different. Of African, Indian, and English heritage, he was born in Pittsburgh the son of a bishop of the African Methodist Episcopal Church. When he was seven, the family moved to Philadelphia, where the AME Church had been founded in 1816. In Philadelphia the talented Tanner was able to study with Thomas Eakins at the Pennsylvania Academy of the Fine Arts from 1880 to 1882, but racial discrimination made it difficult for him to support himself by painting. Consequently, in 1891 he emigrated to Paris to a more welcoming social and artistic milieu. Tanner was elected to New York's National Academy of Design in 1909, but he made Paris his home.

Tanner exhibited in America as well as Europe, and his style was thoroughly Continental. Much influenced by Whistler's poetic landscape manner, Tanner's work also reflects the influence of the French avant-garde. *The Seine*, for example, is strikingly similar to contemporary works by Henri Matisse, who was ten years younger than Tanner. The hazy atmosphere in this painting is suffused with tender color, a peach and rose ground silhouetting the bridge and buildings. The effect of the broad, spontaneous brushstrokes is due in part to the small size of the painting, but this soon became typical of Tanner's art even in large canvases. His style is as evocative of an inner, contemplative world as it is of a particular time of day on the river.

In his most important paintings Tanner used this moody style to portray biblical scenes. The religious stories had inspired his youth and deepened into personal visions as he aged. Of the racial prejudice that drove him out of the country, he remarked: "While I cannot sing our National Hymn . . . still deep down in my heart I love [my country] and am sometimes sad that I cannot live where my heart is" (see Marcia M. Mathews, *Henry Ossawa Tanner, American Artist* [Chicago, 1969]). In the mature art of Henry Tanner, the spiritual roots of an African-American family were wedded to an international language of modern painting to produce highly original works of art.

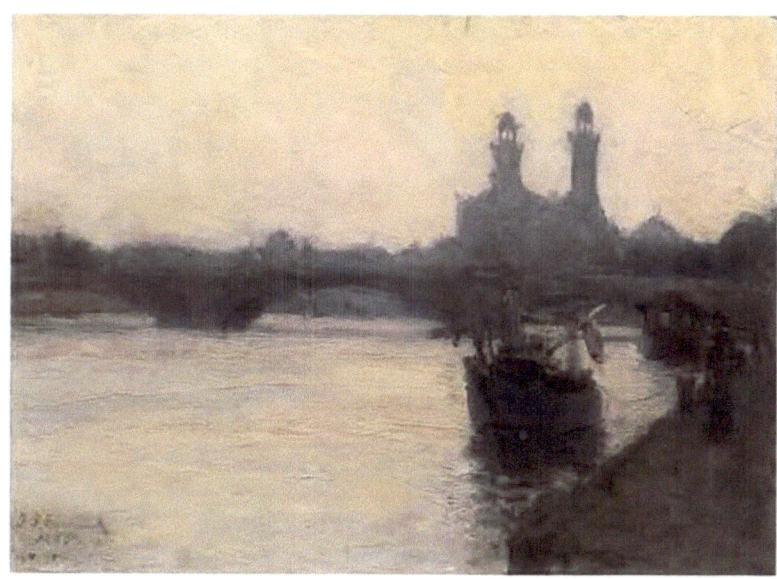

Winslow Homer

Winslow Homer (1836–1910)
Right and Left, **1909**
Oil on canvas, 28¼ x 48⅛ in. (0.718 x 1.229 m)
National Gallery of Art, Gift of the Avalon Foundation

In *Right and Left* one is first struck by the immediacy of the ducks and by the stark but subtle palette of black, gray, and silvery whites against the gradations of predominantly gray water and sky. Homer deliberately balanced the shapes and movements of the ducks in a way that arrests their motion, suspending them before the viewer's eyes. Their arrangement and their closeness to the viewer reminds one of the great prints in John James Audubon's *Birds of America*, while their relatively flat patterns suggest the effect of Japanese prints. Both of these are possible sources, perhaps subconsciously, for the composition.

But Homer was not a naturalist or an illustrator in *Right and Left*. Looking closer at the painting, one glimpses at the crest of a wave in the left background the dim shape of a boat and two men, one seated, the other standing. Then follows the shocking realization that the standing figure is a hunter who has just fired his gun. This shot explains the contrasting positions of the ducks and is the punch line to this short story in paint. The hunter has already fired once, hitting the duck at the right that plummets toward the wave, its black bill echoed by a single whitecap. And the man has just fired a second shot, pos-

sibly hitting the other duck still in its upward flight; its webbed feet are echoed by the pinnate whitecap that reaches up as if to pull the bird down. It is a dance of death that Homer has portrayed, and he has put the viewer squarely in the middle of it—we, like the ducks, are in the line of fire. The title refers to the feat of killing two birds with two blasts, and it was given not by Homer but by a sportsman who saw the painting in a gallery. *Right and Left* is an intensely disquieting painting and a masterpiece of American art.

Homer executed this painting, his next-to-last work, after several years during which he painted little, and after suffering a slight stroke. *Right and Left* must have had great personal significance for the artist, then seventy-three. Homer was as close to nature as a person could be. For more than twenty years he had lived on the harsh Maine coast and spent long months in the Adirondacks or in the Bahamas. Nature was his chosen habitat and his chosen subject in the vast majority of his paintings and watercolors. He was in harmony with the tides, the seasons, and the life cycles of animals and plants. His profound empathy with the laws of nature and a sense of humanity's marginal place in it was like that of Henry David Thoreau, who wrote in *Walden* (1854): "I love the wild not less than the good."

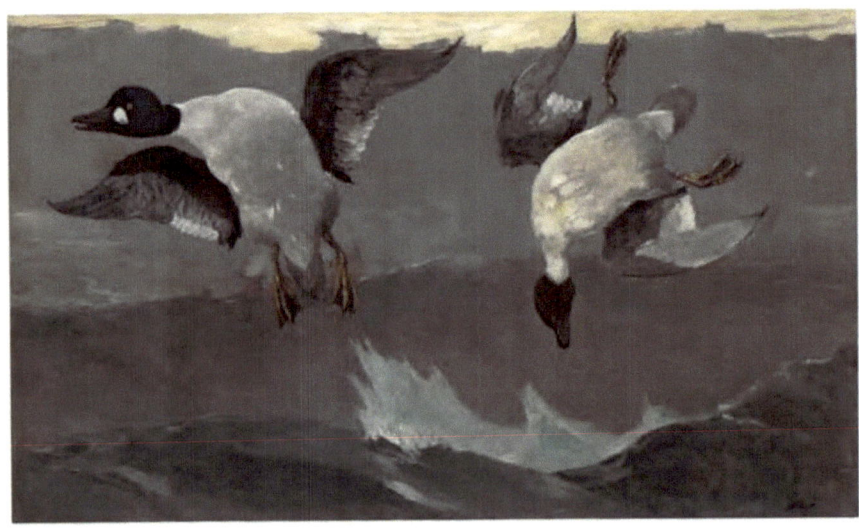

George Bellows

George Bellows (1882–1925)
Both Members of This Club, 1909
Oil on canvas, 45¼ x 63⅛ in. (1.150 x 1.605 m)
National Gallery of Art, Chester Dale Collection

In the same year that Homer painted *Right and Left*, a summation of the American landscape tradition, George Bellows painted *Both Members of This Club*, a physical plunge into the cauldron of the American city. For all the differences in subject matter, however, Bellows' raw masterpiece has much in common with Homer's more restrained painting. Both artists throw the viewer directly into the action: Bellows' fighters are forced upon us as much as Homer's ducks. Both works are about human violence, in Bellows' case between men themselves. In both we are more than viewers, we become witnesses, unwilling participants in the emotional scene.

Bellows' punches are literal rather than metaphorical, however, and the emotion is riotous and extravagant. This is an expressionist painting in which the surging bodies of the fighters and the howling faces of the fight crowd are equally exaggerated—twisted and stretched into writhing muscles and grotesque masks of pure unreason. Thomas Eakins also painted boxing scenes, but his figures appear poised and contemplative in contrast to the visceral energy of Bellows' fighters. In *Both Members of This Club* the black boxer prevails over his opponent with a powerful lunge.

Due to corruption in the sport, public boxing had been prohibited in New York state between 1900 and 1910. Matches were permitted only at private clubs where both spectators and contestants were members. The irony of the painting's title, *Both Members of This Club*, refers to fighters who were granted temporary memberships only for the night of the bout in order to circumvent the law.

Neither the white nor the black boxer would have been considered socially acceptable as a full member of an athletic club. But in that segregated society, private boxing clubs were among the few places where black and white could come together at all.

Besides painting the scenes and, by implication, the issues of American society, Bellows also contributed drawings to the socialist publication *The Masses*. His compassion for the individual in modern society is also evident in his moving, insightful portraits. He was only ten years old when Walt Whitman died, but he has often been compared to him for generosity of spirit. Bellows certainly agreed with Whitman, who in *Song of Myself* (1855) had written: "And I know . . . that all the men ever born are also my brothers, and the women my sisters. . . . / I am the mate and companion of people, all just as immortal and fathomless as myself."

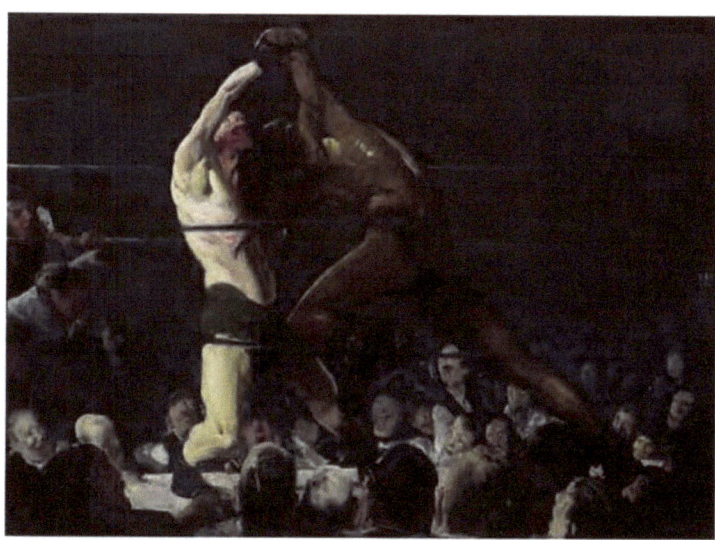

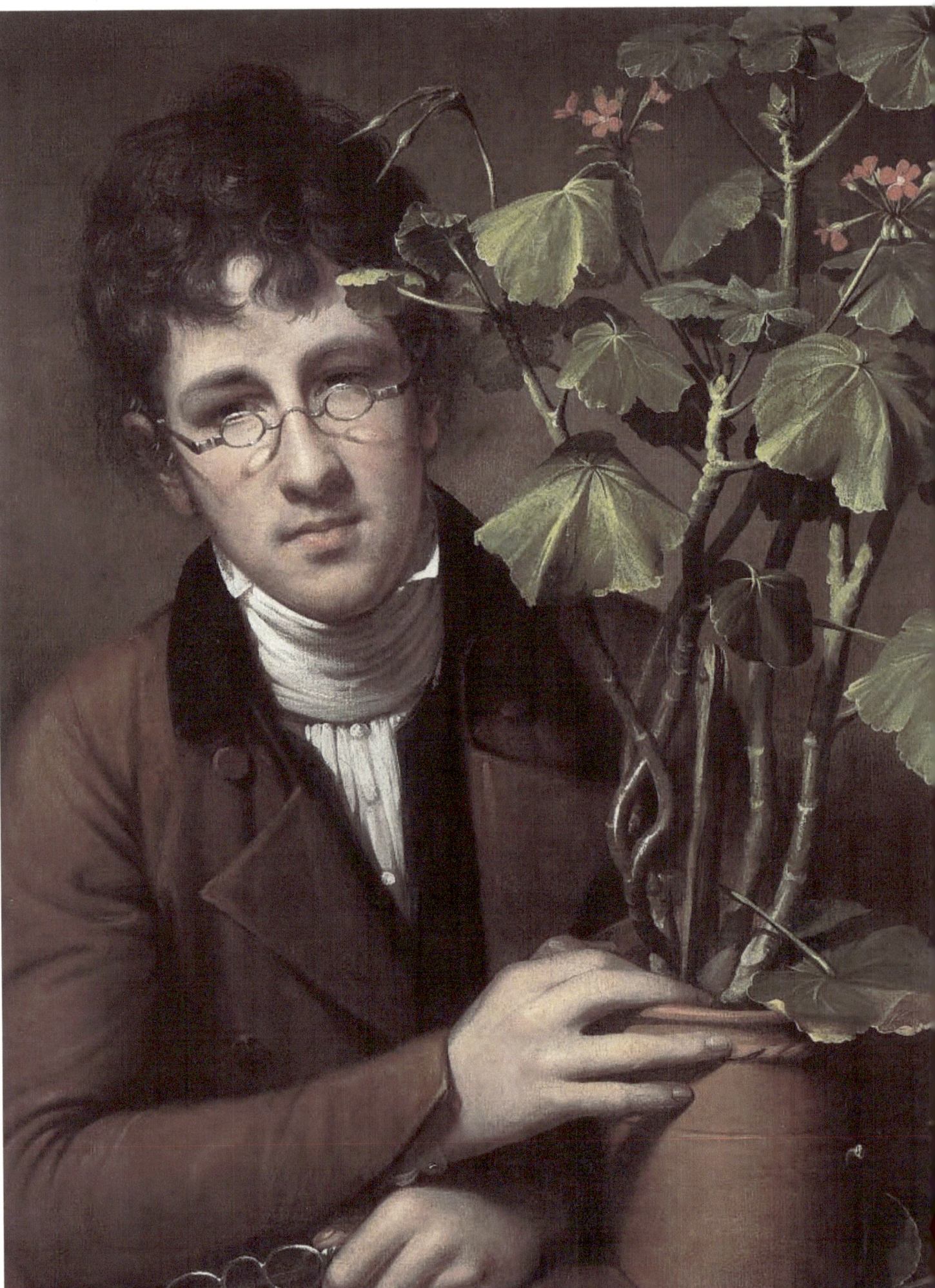

DISCUSSION QUESTIONS AND ACTIVITIES

GENERAL

Display the timeline and discuss important historical events with students. Familiarize students with general historical periods and trends; locate the lifetimes of the artists discussed in this packet on the timeline.

Display the reproductions and/or project the slides in the classroom. Discuss them with your students in terms of subject, style, and emotional expression, first asking for student impressions.

Ask students to identify American subjects in these paintings: people, activities, and places that are characteristically American; themes from American literature.

Using the reproductions, explain to students that paintings have an immediate, physical quality, which artists achieve partly through making us especially aware of our senses: sight, touch, taste, smell, and sound. Group the reproductions by which sense they most exemplify. Discuss how sensual information is conveyed: for example, touch can be shown through different textures of fabrics and surfaces, and by following the "touch" of the artist's hand through the brushstrokes visible in the painting.

Have students study composition by looking closely at a work from each of the following four categories: Portraiture, Looking at Nature, Narrative Art, and People and Places. Discuss the concept of organizing objects in space and the different ways artists accomplish this (triangle, circle, diagonal, etc.). Discuss the importance of composition in creating emphasis, in communicating content, and in moving a viewer's eyes around the picture.

Have students make a schematic drawing of one of the compositions. Notice that even in action scenes with dramatic movement the scene is still clear and stable because of the underlying organization and balance. Have students execute a drawing of a still life, stressing the idea of "composing" the forms and space in their drawings.

Look at the paintings from the perspective of color only. Discuss with or demonstrate to students how an artist uses color to create mood, space (advancing and receding), temperature (warm and cool), and value. Then have students focus on one painting and discuss value, intensity, and emotional expression of colors used. Have students list the colors as descriptively as possible: for example, shades of red as cranberry red, brick red, blood red, fire red, passionate red, etc.

Bring your students to the National Gallery of Art to see the actual paintings, or to a local museum or historic house to experience American art first-hand. Remind them that slides and reproductions may change the size, change the colors, and eliminate texture from the real works of art.

PORTRAITURE

John Singleton Copley, *Epes Sargent*, c. 1760

Gilbert Stuart, *Mrs. Richard Yates*, 1793/1794

Rembrandt Peale, *Rubens Peale with a Geranium*, 1801

Joshua Johnson, *The Westwood Children*, c. 1807

James McNeill Whistler, *The White Girl (Symphony in White, No. 1)*, 1862

Discussion Questions

Beginning

Compare *Rubens Peale with a Geranium* and *The Westwood Children*. Define "attribute" (an object closely associated with, characteristic of, or belonging to a specific person, thing, or office). Point out the attributes in these two paintings and discuss how attributes represent the individuals and add meaning. For example, the roses held by the boys in *The Westwood Children* symbolize the fragility, beauty, and innocence of childhood.

Have students guess how long ago these portraits were painted. What clues are they given by the portraits? Is it difficult to tell the time period for any of the portraits? Why or why not?

Intermediate

Have students guess why and for whom the portraits were painted. Look for clues by examining clothing, pose, and expression. Categorize these clues as informal/formal, direct/indirect, natural/contrived. Are any portraits both private (meant to be enjoyed by someone close to the sitter) and public (meant to show the sitter's—or artist's—prominence)?

Have students look at how the artists emphasize hands and faces in these portraits. Discuss what is revealed about the person by their hands. Relate to students how hands can reveal social status (calluses, gloves), occupation (pianist, auto mechanic), interests (by holding a pen, sewing needle, eyeglasses), personality (gesture, pose), etc. Ask students how they would like their hands to be displayed for a portrait and what they reveal about themselves by their hands.

Advanced

Compare the portraits *Epes Sargent* and *Mrs. Richard Yates*. Both paintings portray compelling personalities. Point out their poses, clothing, and demeanor. Notice how convincing and real these individuals are—Mrs. Richard Yates has just been interrupted at her mending, and Epes Sargent leans heavily on the column with his hair powder dusting his shoulder. What values and character traits can students ascribe to these early Americans (serious, industrious, forthright, capable, no-nonsense, etc.)?

Compare *Rembrandt Peale with a Geranium*, *The Westwood Children*, and *The White Girl*, looking at style. Ask a series of questions to help students identify differences and similarities. What portrait looks the most (or the least) realistic? Why? Why did the artist paint the portrait? What does the manner in which the portrait was painted reveal about the artist? About the person or people represented?

Activities

Beginning　Have students choose attributes that describe them—their personalities, characteristics, and/or their heritage or culture and include them in a self-portrait.

Have students look through magazines and cut out images of people. Assemble the images and create a collage of portraits that express one or two traits or characteristics: for example, confidence, dedication, anger, concentration, etc. Make sure that students include not just faces, but whole figures and their environments if they contribute to that expression.

Intermediate　Have students look at *The White Girl* and *Mrs. Richard Yates* and then make associations with the color white: clean, cold, pure, etc. Develop vocabulary by using synonyms for white: milky, bloodless, snowy, chalky, etc. Collect different shades and hues of white, cutting swatches from magazines and papers. Make a collage with the swatches. Are they all "white"? Do some of the whites recede? Do others advance? Why?

Have students photograph each other, creating a studio portrait by carefully selecting costume, props, pose, and background. Students may want to create a personality or emphasize one aspect of their own character.

Advanced　Assign students to read a biography of a famous American of their choice. With the information they learn from the biography, have students write a soliloquy that reveals the unspoken thoughts and reflections of that person.

Have students make a drawing in the manner of Rembrandt Peale, Joshua Johnson, or James McNeill Whistler. Encourage students to research one of these artists and look at other works by that artist before attempting to work in their style.

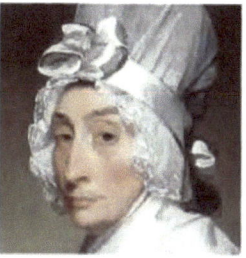

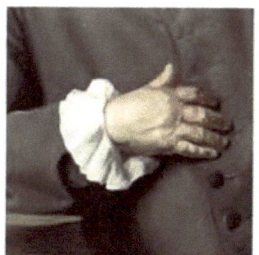

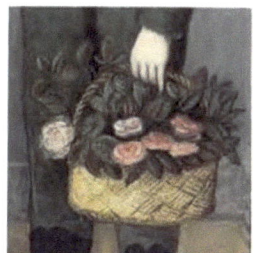

LOOKING AT NATURE

James Peale, *Fruit Still Life with Chinese Export Basket*, 1824

Thomas Cole, *The Notch of the White Mountains (Crawford Notch)*, 1839

George Inness, *The Lackawanna Valley*, 1855

John Frederick Kensett, *Beacon Rock, Newport Harbor*, 1857

Frederic Edwin Church, *Morning in the Tropics*, 1877

Henry Ossawa Tanner, *The Seine*, 1902

Winslow Homer, *Right and Left*, 1909

Discussion Questions

Beginning

Have students identify the season, time of day, and weather for each landscape based on the information given in the painting. For example, in Cole's *The Notch of the White Mountains*, the red and gold leaves of the trees reveal that it is autumn, the long shadows cast by the sun reveal that it is late afternoon, and the dark cloud on the left suggests that a storm is coming.

Have students choose a landscape and discuss how the picture makes them feel. Point out to students that some landscapes elicit a specific emotional response, for example, Church's *Morning in the Tropics*. What does the artist do to evoke a particular mood? Encourage students to be specific in their responses.

Intermediate

Discuss with students what attitudes are reflected toward the land and nature by these paintings: *The Notch of the White Mountains*, *Morning in the Tropics*, *The Lackawanna Valley*, and *Right and Left*. Have any of these attitudes changed in the last one hundred years? Ask students to express their thoughts on contemporary issues dealing with land and nature.

Have students look carefully at *Notch of the White Mountains*, *Right and Left*, *Fruit Still Life with Chinese Export Basket*, and *The Seine*. Ask them to discuss whether the artist was painting an actual scene or inventing one from his imagination and how they are able to tell.

Advanced

Discuss the concept of time in relation to these paintings. Do some of the paintings appear eternal? Are there any that reflect the momentary? What may be the reasons an artist has in conveying a particular attitude about time?

Compare *The Lackawanna Valley*, *Notch of the White Mountains*, and *Morning in the Tropics*, tying these images in with a general picture of American history: exploration of the Americas, settling of the wilderness, and the change from an agrarian to an industrial society. Discuss the implications of these events for the environment and peoples' past way of life. Ask students if they can tell how the artists felt about these changes, which happened during their lifetimes.

Activities

Beginning   Have students formulate a weather report or local news flash based on the weather conditions for that day or in one of the landscape paintings. Have students base their report on careful observation, noting, for example, types of clouds, the strength, temperature, and direction of the wind, and the kind of weather that is typical for the season.

Have students describe the experience of one of these landscapes as if they were there. Or have them describe a landscape that has special meaning for them: a vacation spot, for example, or their backyard. Expand students' vocabulary by giving them a list of adjectives to use in their description: majestic, serene, vast, intimate, tranquil, sensational, dazzling, picturesque, cozy, lush, etc.

Intermediate   Have students cut out newspaper articles on ecology and the environment. Discuss with students both local and international concerns. Have students form a panel and debate the various sides of one issue: preservation of the rain forest, for example, or Native American hunting and fishing rights.

Have students paint a landscape by going outdoors or by using photographs. Ask students to make careful observations in order to create a factual record. Then have students paint this landscape, exaggerating certain elements to create an emotion: terror, reverence, grief, joy, etc. Have students select colors, scale, and the kinds of lines and forms appropriate for the feeling they want to express.

Advanced   Show the class photographs of a landscape that has special meaning to you. Have students write a poem or short story about a landscape they remember, describing the place and their feelings or the event that gives this place meaning. Refer to and familiarize students with works of literature and poetry about landscape: Henry David Thoreau's *Walden*, for example, or Robert Frost's *Stopping by Woods on a Snowy Evening*.

Have students write an essay on their idea of paradise or the perfect place to escape. Have them illustrate their essays. Tell students about the Europeans' vision of America—the New World, a new Eden—and how this vision had an impact on American history (the belief in Manifest Destiny, for example).

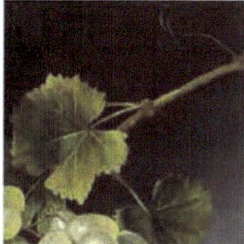 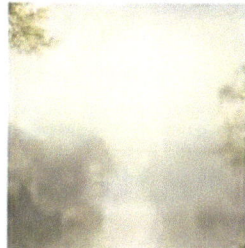 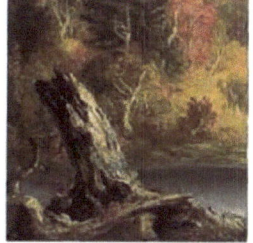

NARRATIVE ART   John Singleton Copley, *Watson and the Shark*, 1778
Edward Hicks, *Peaceable Kingdom*, c. 1834
John Quidor, *The Return of Rip Van Winkle*, c. 1849
Albert Pinkham Ryder, *Siegfried and the Rhine Maidens*, 1888/1891

Discussion Questions

Beginning   Ask students if these pictures make them wonder what is going on? Before telling any of the stories, have students theorize on what is happening in each picture. Discuss the saying, "A picture is worth a thousand words."

Have students point out who is the lead character in each picture. Ask students how the artist emphasizes this character, through placement, gesture, the reactions of the other characters, etc.

Intermediate   Ask students to put words into the mouths of the characters in *Siegfried and the Rhine Maidens*, *Watson and the Shark*, and *The Return of Rip Van Winkle*. Read them the texts that go with these paintings (found in the object entries). Have students analyze how the artist relates the story in each of these paintings without saying a single word.

Have students look at *Watson and the Shark* and *Peaceable Kingdom*. Ask students to speculate why an artist would paint a particular story. Copley painted a replica of *Watson and the Shark* (one was commissioned by Brook Watson to give to an orphanage, and the other Copley kept for himself), and Hicks painted over sixty variations of *Peaceable Kingdom* (Hicks was a Quaker and this scene symbolized his belief in harmony, peace, and freedom in the United States).

Advanced   Discuss with students how the artists painted these scenes, none of which they observed in real life. For example, look at *Watson and the Shark* and *The Return of Rip Van Winkle*. Ask students where they think Copley and Quidor executed their paintings and how the pictures were composed. Discuss the process of making preparatory drawings, using models to get certain poses, and even "borrowing" from other works of art (Copley borrowed from Raphael and Hicks from several popular prints).

Compare the scenes of history and actual events with the scenes from folktales and literature. Ask students if they can tell whether the scene is real or imaginary based on the way the artist has presented it. Have students look carefully at *Peaceable Kingdom*, which combines both history and belief, and discuss the distinction made between imagination and reality.

Activities

Beginning   Have students make a *tableau vivant* (a living picture) of one of these paintings. Afterward ask them what they learned about the painting by enacting the scene. Were the poses natural or awkward? What props did they need?

Have students illustrate a story with one picture relating the most exciting or crucial moment.

Intermediate   The action paintings of *The Return of Rip Van Winkle* and *Watson and the Shark* make past events or stories seem as if they were happening today. Have students present a newscast as if they were a reporter on the scene, or hold an interview with Brook Watson or Rip Van Winkle. Have them write up their report based on clear reporting of facts and events.

Have students draw a series of connected scenes, as in a comic strip. Ask them to choose a story or event that has personal significance: a recurring dream, the first time they rode a bike, etc. Have students put captions under their drawings to explain the story.

Advanced   Have students tell a folktale or perform a dramatic reading, either in small groups or individually. Have them practice the art of storytelling before their performance by working with them on speech patterns and accents, gestures, facial expressions, etc.

Have students select a story or historical event to illustrate. Have students plan their work by making preparatory drawings and experimenting with different backgrounds and figure arrangements. Ask students to adapt their styles and techniques to each type of story.

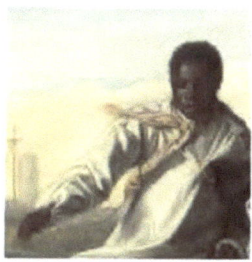

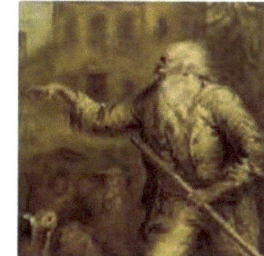

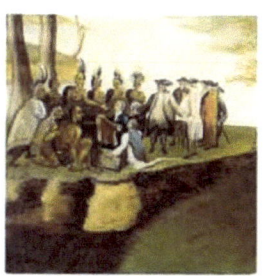

PEOPLE AND PLACES

Thomas Eakins, *The Biglin Brothers Racing*, c. 1873
Winslow Homer, *Breezing Up (A Fair Wind)*, 1876
William Merritt Chase, *A Friendly Call*, 1895
George Bellows, *Both Members of This Club*, 1909

Discussion Questions

Beginning

Discuss the setting for each of these pictures. All of the people are engaged in an activity that requires a particular place, dress, and equipment. Have students identify these things. Discuss what is needed to play baseball, visit a relative, go outside on a rainy day, etc.

Ask students if any of the people in these paintings are talking to each other. Discuss what they might be saying. Have students pretend that they are in one of the paintings. Ask what they are doing? What they are talking about?

Intermediate

Have students analyze the people in these paintings and guess what their relationship is to each other. How do they know if the people are brothers, friends, team members, or antagonists?

Have students look at each of these pictures and find where the viewers are located. How is the viewer included in the scene? Does the viewer have a role to play in any of the scenes (spectator, participant, intruder)?

Advanced

Look at the three pictures *The Biglin Brothers Racing*, *Breezing Up*, and *Both Members of This Club*, which depict people engaged in the sports of sculling, sailing, and boxing. Ask if any of the people are enjoying themselves. Which is the most serious? Which do the students think are amateurs and which are professionals? Why do people "play" sports? Discuss the role sports plays in American life today.

Have students analyze the figure in motion by comparing these four works. Point out the type of symmetry, either translation symmetry (*Breezing Up* and *The Biglin Brothers Racing*) or mirror symmetry (*A Friendly Call* and *Both Members of This Club*). Ask how symmetry can imply repeated and sequential motions. Have students look at stop-action photography for comparison.

Activities

Beginning   Describe to students a sport with which they are unfamiliar, such as croquet, curling, boccie, windsurfing, sumo, etc. Have students design the sporting equipment and arena or playing field necessary for the sport based on your description of the rules and object of the game. Or have students invent their own game or sport.

Have several students assume an action pose. Have the rest of the class draw the grouping. Work with students to avoid strict frontal or profile images; have them attempt to show the figures in three-quarters view or twisting.

Intermediate   Have students write a dialogue for *A Friendly Call* or *Breezing Up*. Have them consider what topics would be appropriate for the situation and the interests of the characters.

Look at the action scenes of *The Biglin Brothers Racing* and *Both Members of This Club*. Have students attend a sporting event and either photograph or sketch the crucial moments to make finished drawings from after the event.

Advanced   Have students make a "flip book" by drawing the same object or person(s) on each page. By slightly changing the positions of the object or person(s) on successive pages, the motions will appear to happen sequentially when the pages are flipped.

Assign students to research the training schedule or life story of a professional or Olympic athlete and write a brief report. Then have students write about their (future) profession. Ask them to describe what training is necessary and what the requirements are for their profession.

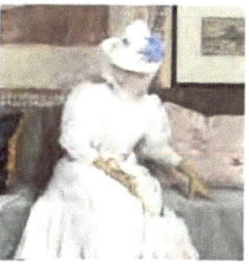

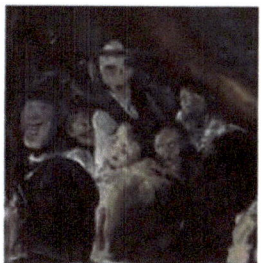

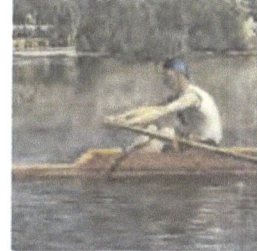

BIBLIOGRAPHY

Baigell, Matthew. *Dictionary of American Art.* New York: Harper & Row, 1979. Not illustrated. [inexpensive paperback]

Brown, Milton W., et al. *American Art: Painting, Sculpture, Architecture, Decorative Arts, Photography.* Rev. ed. New York: Harry N. Abrams, Inc., 1979. The leading full-treatment, lavishly illustrated survey of American art.

Craven, Wayne. *Colonial American Portraiture.* Cambridge and New York: Cambridge University Press, 1986. Nearly 200 black and white illustrations. Fine text.

Craven, Wayne. *Sculpture in America.* New York: Crowell, 1968. Excellent survey of American sculpture.

Flexner, James Thomas. *History of American Painting.* 3 vols. New York: Dover Publications, Inc., 1969. Includes vol. 1, *First Flowers of Our Wilderness (The Colonial Period)*; vol. 2, *The Light of Distant Skies (1760-1835)*; and vol. 3, *That Wilder Image: The Painting of America's Native School from Thomas Cole to Winslow Homer.* These volumes appeared separately between 1947 and 1962. Flexner's text is especially good for its insights and historical awareness. [inexpensive paperback]

Gowan, Alan. *Images of American Living: Four Centuries of Architecture and Furniture as Cultural Expression.* New York: Harper & Row, 1964. A thorough survey and very readable. [inexpensive paperback]

Howat, John K. *The Hudson River and Its Painters.* New York: Viking Press, 1972. [Reissued in 1983 by American Legacy Press, New York.] Concise text covers many artists; 100 illustrations, many in color.

Richardson, Edgar P. *Painting in America.* New York: Thomas Y. Crowell Co., 1956. The first modern comprehensive survey of American art, still one of the best.

Taylor, Joshua C. *The Fine Arts in America.* Chicago and London: The University of Chicago Press, 1979. A literate and thought-provoking interpretation of American art in the full cultural context. [inexpensive paperback]

Taylor, Joshua C. *To See Is to Think: Looking at American Art.* Washington, D.C.: Smithsonian Institution Press, 1975. A book for all levels above the elementary, it is one of the best guides to looking at and thinking about art. Illustrated with art from the National Museum of American Art, it continues into the 1960s.

Taylor, Joshua C. *America as Art.* Washington, D.C.: Smithsonian Institution Press, 1976. [Reissued by Harper & Row, Icon paperback, relatively inexpensive]

Wilmerding, John. *American Masterpieces from the National Gallery of Art.* 2d rev. ed. New York: Hudson Hills Press, 1988. A comprehensive treatment of the National Gallery's American art collection. Sixty-five color plates, many black and white photographs. Includes many of the paintings in this guide.